IN MY SKIN

BRITTNEY GRINER

WITH SUE HOVEY

IN MY SKIN

MY LIFE ON AND OFF THE BASKETBALL COURT

DEY ST.
AN IMPRINT OF WILLIAM MORROW PUBLISHERS

DEY ST.

All insert photographs are courtesy of the Griner family, except for page 4 (*bottom*): Janell Roy; page 5: Julio Trejo; page 6 (*top*): Jesse D. Garrabrant/NBAE; pages 6 (*bottom left*) and 8 (*top*): Phoenix Mercury/Barry Gossage; page 6 (*bottom right*): Barry Gossage/NBAE; page 7: Yoon Sui; page 8 (*bottom*): Nathaniel S. Butler/NBAE.

HarperCollins books may be purchased for educational, business, or sales promotional use. For information please e-mail the Special Markets Department at SPsales@harpercollins.com.

A hardcover edition of this book was published in 2014 by It Books, an imprint of HarperCollins Publishers.

FIRST DEY STREET BOOKS PAPERBACK EDITION PUBLISHED 2015.

Designed by Shannon Plunkett

Title page photograph © by Danielle Levitt/AUGUST

HB 04.26.2024 0140

The Library of Congress has catalogued a previous edition of this title as follows:

Griner, Brittney.
 In my skin : my life on and off the basketball court / Brittney Griner.
    pages cm
  ISBN 978-0-06-230933-4 (hardback) 1. Griner, Brittney. 2. Basketball players—United States—Biography. 3. Women basketball players—United States—Biography. I. Title.
 GV884.G78G75 2014
 796.323092—dc23
 [B]

                          2013050667

ISBN 978-0-06-230935-8 (pbk.)

24 25 26 27 28 LBC 10 9 8 7 6

CONTENTS

PROLOGUE

I don't like saying no.

I have a driving desire to make people happy, to the point that I often tire myself out trying to be everything to everyone, saying yes even when I want to say no. Maybe it's because I've spent much of my life dealing with rejection—the vicious taunts I heard as a kid, the disapproval of my sexuality as I got older—so now I find it hard to turn down others, even in the smallest ways. It actually gets me in trouble sometimes, spreading myself thin with friends or making too many public commitments when what I should be doing is catching my breath and carving out some much-needed alone time.

This part of my personality tends to surprise people. They know me only as the six-foot-eight basketball player, the one who doesn't back down, who plays hard, dunks with authority, and lives openly—the one who likes to challenge how society wants to define her. When I tell someone I'm a people pleaser, I'm often met with a raised eyebrow and a look that says, *Really? I never would have guessed it.* But it's true. I want everyone to feel happy and accepted. And I never want to be the cause of someone else's disappointment, because I know all too well how that particular brand of pain feels.

Of course I mess up plenty, too. What I feel and what I do are sometimes out of sync. I've always held things inside, kept most of my true feelings and emotions packed away. From the time I was a kid, I've dealt with so much hurt this way: swallowing it whole, stacking it inside me, thinking I was strong enough to ignore it and keep a smile on my face. Meanwhile, when I was busy telling myself it didn't matter, the hurt would become sadness, then anger, and eventually it would spill over. This seemed natural to me, coping with the ups and downs of life by stuffing everything away until nothing more could fit, then dealing with all of it coming back up at once, a tidal wave of emotion.

If I've done one thing especially well in the past few years, it's break down the walls I had built. And I've learned something important about myself in the process, especially during my college years at Baylor University. I've learned that my top priority is being true to myself, and making choices that reflect who I am as a person, even if those choices—how I dress, what I talk about, who I surround myself with—make some people uncomfortable.

My desire to live authentically has often been at odds with my need to please. I want to be me, but I also want to make the people around me happy. It's a tug-of-war that has consumed me over the years, but one I'm finally learning to manage.

This constant quest to find the right balance is also a big reason I'm sharing my story, because I think anyone who has ever struggled to walk a different path, while also trying to fit in, can appreciate the difficulty of that journey and the lessons learned along the way. In telling my story, I've come to understand myself on a deeper level, to think about how I can be the best version of myself, not just the version that others want to see.

I still have a lot to learn (big understatement). But learning to be the real me has made everything else seem possible.

IT'S COMPLICATED

The morning of my first WNBA game, I did what I always do when my alarm goes off: I hit the snooze button two or three times. I'm not one of those bounce-out-of-bed types. I'm also not someone who gets nervous before big games. As I was lying in bed, though, slowly waking up, my mind jumped ahead to the afternoon. It was 8 A.M. (give or take a snooze), and in six hours, I would walk to center court and officially tip off my pro career. *Let's get this thing started, people!* The past several months had been a whirlwind of media, travel, and drama— lots of drama—and I just wanted to get out on the floor with the Phoenix Mercury, in front of our fans, and hoop.

But first I had to figure out what to wear. That was the one thing I was nervous about, because you're supposed to look nice when you go to the games, and I didn't want to start my career with a fine. So I woke up my girlfriend, Cherelle, and said, "Hey, I need you to dress me." We decided on a navy blue shirt with white polka dots and a pair of dark Levi's jeans (the skinny kind). But the key, the thing we obsessed about, was the bow tie. I had a new one I wanted to wear, a pinkish-purple color (or purply pink), so we watched some videos to see how to tie it, because my agent had been doing that for me before events. We fussed with it for a while until we got the hang of it, like ten or fifteen minutes, long enough to make me impatient. Then we realized the tie didn't really work with my shirt—it was too big for the collar—and I ended up wearing a pink-and-blue one that was already tied.

In other words, I cheated.

You grow up watching players like LeBron James and Kobe Bryant walk into arenas wearing expensive suits, carrying nice bags, and you can see they're making a statement. It's like they're saying, *This is the person I am outside the jersey. This is who I am without a basketball in my hand.* And this was my chance to make that same kind of statement. I had walked into dozens of arenas wearing generic warm-up suits that said nothing about me, the woman underneath. So I couldn't wait to walk into US Airways Center showing off my own style. *This is me, Brittney Griner.*

Becoming a professional basketball player wasn't just about making money or proving myself. It was about freedom, too. In September of my senior year at Baylor University, I watched the WNBA Draft lottery with friends. We had a little party, just chilling and grilling. And when the Mercury won the top pick, I googled the area code for Phoenix, then called Verizon and said I wanted a new phone number—a 602 number. Everyone kept telling me I was going to be the No. 1 draft pick in 2013, the following spring, and I liked having that extra motivation to make it happen. (I also liked how my new phone number had my jersey number in it. That felt like a sign, when I saw a 42 in there, like everything was falling into place.) Thinking about my future in Phoenix gave me a light at the end of the tunnel, because I knew when I turned pro, I would have more control over the things I said and did. No one could choose those things for me anymore.

It really hit home for me in the locker room before my first game with the Mercury, on Memorial Day against the Chicago Sky. The pieces of my life were steadily clicking into place, and my world felt so much bigger—everything from my new California king-size bed, to our arena, to the contract I had recently signed to play for a club in China after the WNBA season. Even my tattoos seemed bigger. I have a flower on my left shoulder, and a week or so before moving to Phoenix, I got it extended down my arm and added a hummingbird to it. I'd been wearing a sleeve in practice to protect the ink, but when I pulled on my jersey before our game against the Sky, and I looked at that new tat, along with the red stars on my left and right shoulders—the ones I had to cover up when I played at Baylor—I suddenly had this *aha* moment. *Hell yeah, I can show off my tats now! I feel free!* I wasn't constricted anymore or burning up in that long-sleeve T-shirt I wore during my last season in college. I felt as comfortable in my new surroundings as I felt in my skin.

It was hard to believe how much had changed in the two months since I had played a basketball game that really mattered, since I'd stepped onto the court with a lot of people watching and wondering how I would perform. A seventy-seven-foot banner of me was hanging on the side of the Hotel Palomar in downtown Phoenix, just across the street from our arena, and every time I saw it, I was reminded of those giant expectations.

I had spent most of my college career in the spotlight. From the moment I set foot on campus as a Baylor freshman, people said I

5

had the potential to do things no female player had done before, that I had a combination of size (did I mention I'm six foot eight?) and skill never seen in the women's game. But it wasn't until my junior season, when we went 40-0 and won the national championship, that I really started to understand what people meant when they said things like "Brittney Griner can be as good as she wants to be." I didn't even start playing basketball until the ninth grade; by the time I left Baylor, I was a two-time national Player of the Year, a three-time All-American, I held the NCAA career record for blocked shots, and I was the second-leading scorer in women's Division I history. Now here I was in Phoenix, as one of the most highly touted WNBA rookies ever, and a lot of people around the league were predicting we would win the championship in my first season.

No pressure.

As I sat at my locker, my mind drifted back to my last college game, in Oklahoma City, against Louisville in the Sweet Sixteen of the 2013 NCAA tournament. I hadn't allowed myself to think about that game much at all, and still don't, because it makes me feel a little sick to my stomach. For me, our loss to Louisville—one of the biggest upsets in women's tourney history—was about more than just basketball. And I think I lost more than just a game. In a lot of ways, that night represents my entire senior year, which was one big struggle. I was finally coming into my own as an adult, but before I could step forward and be exactly the person I wanted to be in public, before I could say and do the things I wanted to do, on my own terms, I had to go through some serious growing pains with the two main authority figures in my life: my dad, Raymond Griner, and my coach, Kim Mulkey. I love and respect them both, more than they probably know. But if I had to pick just one word to describe my relationship with each of them? Complicated. All caps COMPLICATED.

The court has almost always been a safe place for me, a space where I can rejuvenate myself. It's where I gained confidence in high school, where I started to overcome the emotional pain and loneliness I felt in middle school, when I dealt with relentless verbal bullying (sometimes by fighting back with my fists). So I was excited to step onto the court in Phoenix, because I knew once my pro career officially started—once I was back into the regular routine of hoops—I could truly begin to rid myself of the bad feelings that still lingered from the final moments of my college career. I was also well aware I had raised the stakes for myself, and now I needed to deliver, both on and off the court. In the two months since the Louisville loss, I had been making all kinds of news. Some of the headlines happened without me doing anything, like when Dallas Mavericks owner Mark Cuban said he would consider drafting me into the NBA. But most of the stories centered around my sexuality, after I casually acknowledged I'm gay.

I've always put myself out there, in more ways than one. I knew when I was done playing for Baylor, I was going to be completely open about my sexuality. It's not like I was hiding it in Waco. I had been out to family and friends for years. But nobody in the media asked me about it at Baylor, probably because that topic was blocked before I even knew about it. When you're a college athlete, all media requests go through the sports information director's office, and I think they were especially cautious about me because the school has a policy against homosexuality. So even though I was open about being gay, I couldn't be open on Baylor's time, which is why I have a lot of mixed emotions about my four years there. I loved being a member of the Lady Bears, and the fans were great. But playing for a program and on a campus that denies a large part of my identity was a tough situation to navigate. I spent a lot of time wondering if they supported Brittney Griner the person or just Brittney Griner the basketball player.

I guess you could say my relationship with Baylor is like my relationship with Kim and my dad. It's complicated.

THERE IS AN INTERESTING STORY behind the SI.com video that everyone now sees as my "coming out" moment. I was in New York City for a few days after the WNBA Draft because the league had scheduled a bunch of media obligations for us—me, Elena Delle Donne, and Skylar Diggins, the top three picks in the draft—and one of our last stops was at the offices of *Sports Illustrated,* to shoot a digital video. A Mercury PR staffer was with me, along with Stephanie Rudnick, a publicist from Wasserman Media Group, the agency that represents me. They went over the ground rules with *SI* ahead of time, to make sure everybody was on the same page, and it became clear pretty quickly that *SI's* goal was to discuss sexuality. The video anchor, Maggie Gray, said she wanted to ask me about it, but Stephanie told her the topic was off-limits. We had an arrangement with another outlet (it was ESPN) to tell my full story, to talk in depth about issues that are really important to me. It was okay for *SI* to ask general questions, like everyone else had been doing, but we didn't want to get into specifics right then and there, because I didn't think a digital video with Elena and Skylar was the place to tell my story, and it wasn't fair to them. We were there trying to promote the league, not our personal histories.

Once we were on set, though, I sensed what was coming. I just didn't know when. I remember thinking, *This lady is going to make it about sexuality.* Sure enough, she brought it up, asking why it's supposedly more accepted for female athletes (like WNBA players, she said) to come out than it is for men—a topic that people could spend hours discussing. I was trying to answer as broadly as I could, but it was hard for me because I had made this pact with myself to be 100 percent open once I left Baylor. So I said, "Being one that's out, it's just being who you are. Don't worry about what other people are going to say. Don't hide who you are." I thought I had sidestepped it because I didn't actually say, "Well, Maggie, I'm gay." But that's when she pounced and asked me a very specific question about how I had handled my sexuality. At that point, I was, like, *Agh! I give up!* And I answered directly: "I've always been open about who I am and my sexuality."

I was pissed off when the interview was over. Not because I didn't feel comfortable talking about my sexuality—obviously I do—but because I wanted to tell my own story and give it the context I thought it deserved, the way Jason Collins got to tell his story when he came out later that month, on the cover of *Sports Illustrated*. I didn't get to do any of that in the little digital video. I felt like they just wanted their breaking news story: "Brittney comes out to *SI*."

When the video went up, everyone made it seem like that was my big Oprah sit-down, my coming-out confession. I was blown away by that reaction. I was following it all on Twitter and thinking, *Hello, people! I'm already out!* Anyone who didn't know just wasn't paying attention. I mean, my Twitter bio had the word *equality* in it and a photo I did for the NOH8 campaign. I had also recently committed to doing a video for the It Gets Better Project and had posted about it on Facebook. It's not like I was going to send out a press release letting everyone know I'm gay; it's my life, and I should get to choose when and how I want to talk about it to the media. In fact, I had already alluded to being gay a couple of days before the SI interview, when I spent time with a *USA Today* reporter on draft day for a story about bringing change to the WNBA. We had the same ground rules as I did with *Sports Illustrated*, so when I mentioned "coming out" to my parents in high school, *USA Today* didn't make a big deal of it, because it was part of a larger point about the importance of being authentic. If

9

you go back and look at the article, which ran a day before the *SI* video, I actually said a lot more to *USA Today* than I did to *SI*, but people didn't jump all over that "news" and try to say I just came out—which goes to show you it's all about how the story is framed. And when it comes to dealing with gay athletes, the media still has a long way to go. As athletes, as people, we want to show who we are and how we think and what makes us tick, but far too often we get reduced to a headline. It's no wonder more athletes don't come out.

I was still annoyed by the whole thing a few days later, especially when I scrolled through Twitter and Instagram. The trolls were saying all the usual crap, but with a new twist: "How can she be a lesbian if she's a man?" and "Of course she likes girls—she has a penis!" I have a love-hate relationship with social media. On the one hand, it provides a sense of community and support; on the other hand, it gives a megaphone to people spouting cruelty and hatred. Like many things in life, the bad comes with the good. And there was plenty of bad, nasty stuff online after the *SI* video hit.

But then I started hearing from more and more people who were telling me, "Hey, you're doing a good thing." It really clicked for me when I was back in Waco about a week later. President Obama spoke during a memorial service on the Baylor campus, for victims of the fertilizer plant explosion in West, Texas. There were EMTs and firefighters all over town that day, coming to pay their respects. And the EMTs from West happened to be right in front of my apartment complex. When I went outside, I was spotted immediately, and they all wanted to take pictures with me. One of the stations seemed to have a number of gays and lesbians on staff, and a man came up to me and started thanking me. He was almost crying. He told me my "coming out" was going to make things better. He also told me there was a local church that was giving them a hard time for being gay. He said they hadn't smiled in weeks, and yet here they were, smiling ear to ear while talking to me.

That moment touched me. I thought, *Okay, what I'm doing really does matter. I'm helping in some way.* By the time I sat down for my big on-camera interview with ESPN a few weeks later and the editors put me on the cover of their magazine, I didn't care that some people were still tweeting stuff like "Brittney Griner just came out to ESPN." I'll come out over and over again if it's a positive thing for gay kids who are struggling with the same stuff I struggled with when I was younger. Because every voice matters, and being different is a good thing. Who wants to be the same as everybody else?

Not me. When I pulled on my Phoenix Mercury uniform before my first game as a pro, looking at those tattoos that everybody was about to see, I thought about how far I had come—and how different everything would be going forward.

11

THE TRUTH ABOUT BACON

My first three days in Phoenix were rough. I can laugh about it now because it seems like a little hiccup in hindsight, but I wasn't laughing at the time. I was a big pathetic lump in the middle of the desert, feeling out of place. Everything had been moving crazy fast for me, and then—bam!—it all stopped, and I was stuck in a holding pattern, looking around at unfamiliar surroundings and thinking, *This is my new life. Welcome to adulthood.* My apartment was about fifteen minutes from downtown, in a gated complex, as part of team housing. It was nice and came fully furnished, but none of my stuff was there yet because I shipped it all, so I had only the things in my suitcase, and most of those were dress clothes. I'm not sure what fancy events I was planning to attend, because the only place I ended up going was my own pity party. I didn't know anybody in Phoenix yet—training camp was still a few days away—and I just felt so sad and alone. I might as well have been on the moon. My phone was my only connection to the world, to my old life. I would call my girlfriend and say, "I want to come back to Waco."

I didn't sleep in my bed the first three nights I was there, because it didn't feel like my bed yet. I just slept on the couch in the living room and watched TV. I was flipping channels and found this show where this dude goes to crazy areas of the world and tries to survive in the wilderness: *Man vs. Wild*. He was stranded on an island somewhere, and I was lying there on the couch, talking at him. "I feel the exact same way, mister. I'm a castaway in this apartment. I'm alone just like you!" It was probably the worst thing for me to watch.

I kept telling myself everything would be fine once my stuff arrived and I met all my teammates. And I'm happy to say it was; Phoenix was a good landing spot for me. But that didn't make those first few days any easier. The hardest part was being so far away from my friends and family back in Houston, especially my mom. I would call her to check in, and I could hear the sadness in her voice, the lump in her throat. I knew she was missing me. She is very emotional. Ever since she was diagnosed with lupus, after my freshman year at Baylor, we've been really close, and I've tried to be strong for her. But I wasn't feeling strong right then. I didn't even want to call her, because it hurt to hear her hurting. At one point, my second night in Phoenix, she called me, and I just sat there on the couch, looking at my phone and thinking, *Nah, can't do it. Can't do it. I'll call her back later.*

I feel guilty remembering that now, because my mom is the one person who has always been there for me, no matter what, loving me without question, just giving and giving. She wouldn't describe herself as strong—in fact, she was sick a lot when I was growing up, in a lot of physical pain, serious back problems—and yet she has always been my rock. She has always let me be me, let me figure out who I am, when so many other people were telling me who I *should* be. I have never felt judged by her. Never.

OF COURSE, LIKE A LOT of kids, I took that for granted when I was younger, how patient my mom was with me. Let me tell you, I gave her hell. For one thing, I had a lot of energy; I couldn't sit still for very long. I was always into something, running around outside, chasing squirrels, digging up worms, climbing trees. But the thing I did best was pushing her buttons, trying to see how much I could get away with when my dad was at work.

I spent a lot of time occupying myself as a kid. We lived in the Bellewood section of Houston until I was in seventh grade. We had a one-story three-bedroom house on a cul-de-sac in a good neighborhood. My father was a cop with the Harris County Sheriff's Office (as I got older, he worked a number of law enforcement jobs), and my mother stayed at home, taking care of me and my sister and the house. My parents are both from Texas. They met when Mom was a cashier at a Houston grocery store and Dad was doing security work there. He had a son and a daughter from his first marriage, and they were around a lot, because Dad was on good terms with his ex-wife. But my brother, DeCarlo, is seventeen years older than me, and my sister SheKera is ten years older. They have always been great to me, and we consider each other full blood, but it's not like we were all running around the yard, playing games, living under the same roof. It was just me and my sister Pier, who's five years older, and the two of us could not be more different. We're much closer now than we were then. Pier was a total girly girl, and I was all rough-and-tumble. She was always in the house, talking on the phone, playing with dolls, watching *Saved by the Bell*, while I was outside wrestling with the dog in the mud. Pier didn't like playing with me because I would usually end up doing something to make her cry. The little sister beat up the big sister.

My mom and I had our bonding moments, but it wasn't like it is now. She taught me how to sew, and I would curl up on her lap in the living room while she watched her favorite shows: *The Price Is Right* and *Family Feud* and anything on the Food Network. I love my mom's cooking. We were big meat eaters in our family, and every night we would have delicious ham or fried chicken or steak or burgers. And yes, I ate a lot of bacon for breakfast. That was something the media latched onto when I was at Baylor—"BG Loves Bacon"—and I played along with it because it felt like one of the few safe topics I could talk about. But I really do love bacon, and nobody knows that better than my mom.

When I was little, I was impossible to wake up in the morning. I was just one of those kids (and then teenagers) who would mumble and roll over and never wake up when someone first called to me. I would yell, "I'm up!"—and then I'd close my eyes and go back to sleep. Sometimes Pier would come in to wake me up, and her go-to move was to shake me, which she knew I hated. Who likes to be woken up that way? As retaliation, I would flail my arms while turning over in my bed, occasionally smacking her as she leaned down to poke at me. One time, when I thought Pier was trying to wake me, I shot my arm out while my eyes were still closed, and I clocked my mom in the head. I didn't hurt her, but I startled her enough that she didn't take any chances after that day. She would just stand in the doorway and call my name—"Brittney, Brittney, wake up!"—until she saw me finally sit up in bed. Eventually she discovered she didn't even have to leave the kitchen to get me up. All she had to do was sizzle some bacon in the skillet, and as soon as I smelled it, I was out of bed and on my way to the breakfast table.

Now fast-forward to my career at Baylor. When we were playing at home, we ate all our pregame meals at Georgia's, this great place in Waco. If we had a night game, I would always get chicken—a thigh and a leg—and a biscuit. If we had a day game, we would eat breakfast there, and I would get French toast and bacon, every time. One game during my freshman year, when we were on our run to the Final Four, all I had for the pregame meal was a big platter of bacon. That afternoon, I played really well, maybe my best game of the season, and Coach Mulkey jokingly said afterward, "Whatever you ate, keep doing it." I'm not sure if she expected me to actually answer her, but I did; I told her I had a lot of bacon. From that day forward, our support staff made sure there was bacon at every team breakfast, including on the road. By my senior year, even the national media would ask me about bacon, and the whole thing became an inside joke with me and my teammates—the bacon sound bite. Whenever a reporter mentioned it, I would play along, especially for on-camera interviews. The anchor would ask, "Did you have bacon today?" And I would flash a big grin and say, "I sure did!"

I'VE ALWAYS HAD a mischievous streak. My mom is really quiet and reserved, sweet and soft, and when I was a kid, I liked to see how much I could get away with on her watch—partly because my dad had so many damn rules, but also because I'm stubborn like him. I had to do all my acting out when he wasn't around. One time, my mom sent me to my room for disobeying, and I climbed out the window, scooted down to the ground, then walked around to the front of the house and rang the doorbell. When she opened the door, I just stood there and said, "Hi. I'm out." She was so mad, she actually started yelling, which is out of character for her. Usually when I was pushing my luck, being a smart mouth, all Momma had to say was, "I'm going to call your father." That's when I would answer, "Okay, I'm going to my room now. Please don't call him!" She never spanked me, but he did. I got the belt sometimes, mostly the hand—although his hands are so big, they felt like a belt.

When my dad was at work, I couldn't go anywhere. The other kids in the neighborhood were riding around on their bikes, but I was supposed to stay in the yard, where my mom could see me. My dad had a very strict upbringing, and that's how he raised me, as if danger lurked around every corner. It didn't help that my brother got into a lot of trouble when he was younger, hanging with the wrong crowd. I couldn't even go over to a friend's house; there were no sleepovers or slumber parties for me. Hell, no. My dad didn't even like the idea of me playing with other kids.

Mom covered for me a lot when I got a little older. Dad would call in the afternoon and ask, "What's Brittney doing? Can I talk to her?" And if I wasn't there, she'd say, "Oh, Baby Girl is sleeping right now," or tell him I was busy doing homework. Meanwhile I was probably down the block, hanging out at the corner store. She saved me a lot of whoopings. I guess it was just easier to disappoint my mother than my father, because I was such a daddy's girl, from the moment I could walk. Everywhere he went, I was there, attached to his leg. He could not get out of the house without me knowing about it. If he was leaving to run an errand, I was in that truck with him. If he was working in the yard or the garage, I was right there next to him. Cutting the grass, putting up a fence, fixing cars, doing repairs around the house—I was Daddy's Little Helper. I learned all about tools in that garage. He'd be working on something, and he'd say, "Go get me a 716 D socket and an extension cord." So I'd go get whatever he wanted.

My mom could never put me in a dress because I would mess it up so fast. She'd put the little lace socks on me, and I'd rip the lace off to make them look like regular socks. We'd go school shopping, and I always ended up in the boys' section because I liked those clothes better. She'd pick something out for me in the girls' section, then hold it up and ask, "Don't you want a new dress for the school year?" And I'd say, "Nope, I'm good."

"What about a skirt?"

"No thank you."

"How about this pretty pink blouse?"

"I like this T-shirt better."

She wasn't going to make me wear something I didn't like, so I got to pick out my own stuff. And my dad didn't care what I wore—at least not back then. He knew I couldn't be outside helping him do stuff if I was in a dress or a skirt. I had this orange shirt with punk rock characters on it, and I wore it all the time. I practically wore it ragged, until it got too tight on me. I also had a pair of overalls I lived in. I wore one strap up, one strap down. I thought I was so cool. (I wasn't.) And I loved being a little rebel.

My best friend when I was eight years old was Thunder, our police-trained rottweiler. We got him after our dog Rottie passed away. Dad liked rottweilers because they're good for protection. I went to a training class with him before we brought Thunder home, and I remember thinking, *That is one mean dog.* I was only allowed to go near Thunder only if Dad was around. We had a fence in the backyard, and Dad put him out there every morning before he went to work. He would tell me, "Do *not* go in that backyard. The dog will bite you." I guess some kids would have been scared when they heard that, but Rottie had never hurt me, and Thunder seemed to like me, too, especially when I slipped him bacon through the fence. After he had been with us for a few weeks, I was curious to see how he would treat me when my father wasn't standing guard over us. One day, while Dad was at work and Mom was busy doing laundry, I looked out the window and saw Thunder on the far side of the yard, away from the house. So I went out there and walked in the opposite direction, to the other side of the yard. I got down on the ground, on my knees, then looked at Thunder. Sure enough, he took off running toward me, full speed. I was so far away from the back door, I could have been mauled. But Thunder did what I thought he would and slid right into my arms.

A little while later, Dad got home and came running outside when he saw me and Thunder rolling around, playing. At first I thought he was going to yell at me, but instead he said, "How the heck did you get him to do that?" I smiled and said, "I don't know. I guess I'm just good with dogs." I didn't tell him I had bacon in my pocket and I'd been giving it to Thunder. I think I knew, instinctively, being close to Thunder was another way of being close to my dad, even as I was trying to assert my independence—in whatever ways an eight-year-old can express free will.

When I wasn't shadowing my father, I was mimicking my brother. I worshipped DeCarlo. I would call him and say, "Come over and spend the night, please!" And when I heard his motorcycle pull up, I'd run outside, jumping up on him, jumping on his bike. I wanted to be just like him. He was into cars, so I was into cars. He had tattoos, so I got them when I was older. I even tried to walk the way he walks. Everything about him seemed adventurous, probably because he's a jack-of-all-trades. He has been a mechanic and a truck driver, worked on oil rigs, installed pools—whatever blows his way. My dad liked how good DeCarlo was to me, but he didn't want me taking after him, because my brother was wild when he was a teenager, doing stupid stuff like boosting cars. He gave my dad hell, and they bumped heads a lot. I remember one time Dad told me and Pier, "There's no bail money for y'all because your brother used it up. So you'd better not end up in jail, because you'll be stuck there."

I thought that was funny as hell, because when you're a kid, you don't fully understand the consequences of your actions, how one mess-up can lead to another, and all of a sudden you find yourself on the wrong path. My dad wanted to make sure I stayed on the right path as I got older, and I appreciate that now. But he would end up saying and doing a lot of things in the years to come that made me question his approach and caused me a lot of pain.

21

A KID GOING NOWHERE

I don't remember the exact moment, the first time I realized I was different from other kids. Because we're all different, right? We're all unique. And everybody always talks about how we should celebrate the things that make each of us special in our own way. The problem is, a lot of people are full of crap when it comes to following their own advice. They say one thing, then do another. They say it's important for kids to express themselves, but from the moment that starts to happen, from the moment kids start to make choices—what clothes they want to wear, what toys they want to play with, what activities they want to pursue—society tries to define them and put them into neat little boxes. Girls are supposed to act this way, boys that way. And any kid who doesn't fit into one of those boxes gets labeled as weird or strange or different.

I guess I started feeling different when everybody started telling me I was. At home, I was a carefree, curious, mischievous little girl. At school, I was a freak. And no matter how much love I got at home, it couldn't protect me from what was happening at school. It couldn't keep me from feeling sad, frustrated, angry, lonely. Everything was getting harder, and I went from being fearless to scared.

As far back as I can remember, I was never attracted to boys. They were just my buddies. I always liked girls. I had a crush on my best friend when I was in elementary school. We would hold hands, like kids do, and I remember thinking it felt good—it felt right. But over the next few years, most everything else started feeling wrong. I'm not sure middle school is easy for any kid; for me, it was awful. I wasn't one of the cool kids, with the trendy new shoes and clothes, and I was starting to stick out more because of my height and appearance. I was all elbows and knees and rough edges. So I just tagged along with my own little group at school and tried to fit in however I could, hoping to avoid the verbal darts that kids were throwing at each other more often. It seems so stupid when I look back on it now, how much I wanted to be part of the in-crowd. You know what? Screw the in-crowd. Trying so hard to be like everyone else, to talk and act like everyone else, to be something you're not, is exhausting and self-destructive. I learned that lesson the hard way, because sixth, seventh, and eighth grades—the years I tried the hardest to fit in—were the worst for me.

I always had a handful of friends. In elementary school, that was all I needed, because it's not like kids are making plans outside of school without their parents. But as I got older, the friends I did have started hanging out together after school, meeting at the mall to walk around, look in the stores, eat pizza at the food court. At first I would ask my dad for permission to join them: "Can I go to my friend's house?" And he would quickly say no, without even really considering it, his voice like a rock dropping. "I don't know anything about that family," he would tell me. "They could be killers." He actually said this; that's how much he distrusted other people and wanted me to learn to do the same. I wasn't allowed to do anything but go to school and come home from school. If I wanted to go to the mall with my friends, he would have been right there with me, like a bodyguard. My mom would let me do what I wanted, but when it came to giving me permission to leave the house, she would always say, "Ask your dad." And after a while, I wouldn't even bother asking him; I'd just trudge away, my disappointment morphing into anger. Pretty soon other kids stopped asking me to hang out, because everyone already knew the answer. I became the "at-school friend."

Anxious to find my place, I started acting like the class clown. I enjoyed trying to make people laugh, because it gets them talking with you. I was often by myself at home, so I fed off whatever energy I could create at school, even if it got me in trouble. I remember one incident from sixth grade that pretty much sums up the way I was behaving. I was sitting at my desk, my classmates all around me, and I decided to start mouthing off to the teacher. If she asked a question, I would call out, "You already know the answer, so why are you asking us?" My classmates were laughing, which only encouraged me more. Finally, after a few of these outbursts, the teacher decided she'd had enough. In front of everyone, she looked at me and said, "I'm going to call home." I didn't believe her, so I said, "Go ahead, call my house. I don't care." Then I methodically called out my home phone number to the teacher, turning around in my chair when I was done to slap hands with the kids behind me.

25

I felt untouchable, right up until the moment the teacher actually picked up the phone on her desk and started dialing the number. I couldn't believe it. She was calling my house, right then and there, with me in the room, in front of everybody. I wanted to keep acting cool, but my heart started thudding in my chest and my head was spinning. What if my dad answered? I knew it was his day off. I said a quick prayer that my mom would pick up the phone and save me. But then I heard his deep, booming voice coming through the receiver. He must have asked to speak to me after the teacher told him how I was misbehaving, because she held out her hand and offered the phone to me. I was trembling as I walked to the front of the room. I slowly took the phone from her.

"Hey, Dad," I said quietly.

"So you're acting up?"

"Uh . . . uh . . ." I stammered, and before I could finish, he cut me off.

"That's enough," he said. "I'll deal with your ass when you get home."

Then he hung up. *Click.* I handed the phone to my teacher and slunk back to my chair. I didn't say a thing the rest of the day, dreading what was to come. That afternoon, I asked the bus driver to drop me off at the end of her route, instead of at the beginning. But all that did was delay the inevitable. After I got off the bus, I circled our house, entering through the back door and sneaking into my room to do homework, to make it seem like I was really busy and focused. My dad wasn't fooled. He was sitting in the living room, and when he heard me, he came straight to my room. That's when all hell broke loose. I tried darting away from him, but he caught me and gave me the spanking he had promised—the hand mixed with the belt.

I WAS A MESS OF emotions in middle school. I could see my classmates were finding their place in the social structure, but I felt adrift, alone, scrambling to figure it all out. My dad wanted me to live inside a glass box, tucked safely away inside our house, exposed to nothing, including the typical interactions kids need. I rebelled by acting like a fool at school, desperate for attention. And as the months passed, I realized I was different from other kids in more ways than one.

The teasing and mocking, the verbal bullying, began some time in sixth grade. I was at Humble Middle School now, with lots of new faces, and I was at least a few inches taller than most girls in my class, but not developing in the same ways they were. I felt like a physical misfit, my body flat and thin, my voice low—a combination that gave my classmates all the ammunition they needed. Most of us were always testing each other in some way, teasing, making cracks, the typical kid stuff at that age. But as we settled into our surroundings, the interactions grew more cruel.

Soon enough, I became a regular target.

The first time it happened, I was walking with a friend between classes. The hallways were flooded with kids, all of us buzzing as we scurried around like animals freed from a cage. Then suddenly, out of nowhere, one of the Cool Girls was standing in front of me. I could see her friends gathered off to the side, watching, as if they had all been talking about something. Then this girl started patting my chest. I always wore really plain clothing, like a white T-shirt without any graphics on it, and my hair was pulled back in a tight bun. Instinctively, I stepped back, startled and confused. She immediately turned to her friends and said, "See? I told you. She doesn't have a chest!" Then they all walked off, laughing, and I heard one of them say, "She must be a boy. She's not really a girl."

This kind of thing started happening all the time. Somebody would come up close, in my space, and call me names. They'd say things like "What are you, some kind of freak?" Or they'd walk by and say to each other, real loud, "Better watch out—she'll make you gay!" They were constantly making fun of how I looked and dressed, how I walked and talked. I'm not sure I can express exactly how I felt in those moments, because I usually went numb. When you're on the receiving end of insults every day, they chip away at your self-esteem. No matter how much you try to ignore it or tell yourself it's just kids being stupid, you can't avoid the pain that comes with it. You get to a point where you imagine everyone is looking at you and thinking there's something wrong with you. Whenever we had class changes, I would walk with a friend, never alone, always on the lookout for certain girls who made it a habit to harass me. It was almost always girls. I would try to duck them, just get to where I was going as fast as possible, but when somebody got in my face, I got mad. I'd push the girl away and keep walking, as the anger rose inside me. And then I would often act out later in the day, saying something rude to a teacher or cutting another kid down with a nasty comment. It became a terrible cycle, how I passed along that meanspirited behavior, ruining someone else's day to match what was happening to me. It was like a twisted game of Pay It Forward.

During those years, whenever I imagined my future, I pictured myself enlisting in the military after high school. College was just something that other people did; it wasn't part of my plan at all. And sports weren't a factor for me yet. I started dabbling with soccer and volleyball in seventh grade, but the only thing I knew about basketball was that my sister SheKera had played it in high school. I wanted to follow in my dad's footsteps, and that started with joining the military, just as he had done when he was eighteen. After I served, I would pursue a career in law enforcement,

28

same as him. (People might find this hard to believe, but I still think about becoming a police officer someday, when I'm done playing hoops for a living.) The point is, there was nothing going on in my life forcing me to focus on my behavior, to make me think about how my actions in middle school might affect my future. Quite honestly, I viewed what was happening at this time—all the confrontations, the emotional beating I was taking, the tough exterior I was developing—as preparation for the military and police work. There's not a lot of clearheaded thinking when you're in sixth grade, especially when you're carrying around so much anger.

I began to think the only way to make it all stop was if I forced kids to stop, if I made them see I was ready to fight anyone who cut me down; then they would leave me alone. Obviously I realize the flaws in that thinking now, but at the time I thought it was absolutely necessary I be seen as someone you wouldn't want to mess with. The tougher I seemed on the outside, the less likely it was that anyone would see how I was crumbling on the inside. So I allowed my anger to get the best of me.

Until middle school, I would just get in harmless little skirmishes with boys on the playground or in the lunchroom, over silly things. One time in elementary school, I got sent to the principal's office after scuffling with a boy who was mad that I was bragging about beating him in the Punt, Pass, and Kick competition. (Girls and boys competed separately, but I made sure to keep score, and I brought my trophy to school.) Those tussles were nothing compared to the trouble I ran into a few years later. In sixth grade, I got into a full-fledged fight with one of the girls who kept messing with me—a fight that ended with me being sent to an alternative school, basically a reform school, for two weeks. There had been a lot of tension between me and this girl for a while, because she didn't like that I was hanging out with the

29

boys. She was convinced I had a crush on her boyfriend, and she kept threatening me, saying things like "If you try to mess with him, I will come after you. I'm tired of seeing your ugly-ass face in the hall." She was telling other girls to keep an eye on me, that I couldn't be trusted. This was my life at the time: I made some girls nervous because they thought I looked like a boy, and I made other girls nervous because they thought I wanted to steal their boys. But nobody was more nervous than I was, because I was constantly on edge, wondering who was going to provoke me next. My anxiety and anger were fueling each other, and eventually I just exploded.

I was eating lunch one day, sitting with a friend, and I saw the girl walk into the cafeteria. As soon as she set foot in there, I knew she was heading directly for me. I nudged my friend and said, "Here she comes!" And my friend, who was probably nervous, too, said, "Oh, she's definitely coming!" I jumped out of my seat and stood as tall as I could. Sure enough, the girl came up to me and started jawing at me. She was standing so close I could feel her breath. So I took my hand and mushed her face back. That's the best way I can explain it; I covered her face with my palm and pushed her. Well, you can imagine what happened next. When she regained her balance, she came at me swinging, and I didn't back down. This was the whole point of the moment: to show everyone how tough I was.

We became a tangled ball of flailing arms and legs. One of the lunchroom monitors, a member of the school support staff, tried to break us up, but I was so wrapped up in the moment, I shoved him out of the way. A minute later, the school cops showed up and got between me and the girl, holding us down so we couldn't keep fighting. I was sent straight to the principal's office, a place I was pretty familiar with, thanks to my habit of mouthing off to teachers. This situation was much worse than usual, though, because I had pushed a school employee. I was given a misdemeanor ticket and had to appear in juvenile court, where I was sent to reform school, put on probation, and ordered to do community service. (I walked dogs at PetSmart for a few months.)

I didn't feel like I had a choice when it came to fighting. My father had always told me, "Don't start a fight, but don't walk away if someone comes at you—or else you'll get hit in the back of the head." And I was too scared to tell my parents or my teachers about all the name-calling, because I couldn't even begin to verbalize it. Saying the words out loud would only make them more painful. I already felt different, like there was something wrong with me. Why give anyone else a reason to think it might be true? I had no idea how to express all the emotions swirling in my head, and no confidence that anyone could change the situation. I would walk around school with my fists clenched, trying to squeeze away the anger. And every day when I got home, I would retreat to my room, the only place where I could let my guard down, where the anger gave way to the sadness underneath.

I HAVE SOME GOOD MEMORIES of my childhood bedroom. The floor next to the dresser was covered with my favorite toys, including the stuffed animals that my dad had won for me playing arcade games. (He was really good at the one where you have to maneuver the big claw to grab a prize.) Next to those were the Hot Wheels and G.I. Joes I played with when I was really little. My mom had bought me Barbie dolls at some point, but I cut off all their hair and painted them green and black, which I'm sure will surprise no one. My twin-size bed was tucked into the corner, and there was one really big window facing our yard and the road beyond it. I had a small TV on top of my dresser; my Nintendo and Xbox were hooked up to it. I might have been the laziest kid in Houston, because at some point I had lost the remote control for the TV, so I kept a pool stick next to my bed, and I would use it to click the buttons on the console instead of getting out of bed to change the channel. My parents made me turn off the TV at a certain time of night, but once they checked on me, I would often turn down the volume all the way and continue playing my games, keeping one ear focused on the noises coming from the living room. If I heard the creaking of my dad's chair, I would quickly press power on all the devices and flop back into bed. (Funny how I didn't need my pool stick then.)

But I also had some of my lowest moments inside that room. I would often sit on the carpeted floor between the bed and the dresser, drawing pictures and writing stories, trying to make sense of what was happening at school, how I was constantly being ridiculed for the way I looked. I had a lot of time to myself during those middle-school years, long afternoons that dragged on into longer nights. I was under strict orders from my dad to come directly home after school, so I had hours to occupy myself when I wasn't doing homework—time that many of my friends were spending with each other, busy being the "normal" kids I so desperately wanted to become. Sometimes at night I would lie in bed thinking about the same things over and over, wondering what the heck was wrong with me, crying into my stuffed animals. When it was really bad, and I couldn't sleep because my brain was on an endless loop, I would take out a spiral notebook that I hid under my mattress or stuffed inside a game box beneath my bed. It was the same notebook I buried myself in when I got home from school, drawing and writing, and now I would scribble all my thoughts and questions: *Why am I so different? Why can't I be like everyone else? Will I ever be happy? Please just make me normal when I wake up.* The irony, of course, is that I was wishing away so much of what would eventually make me successful at basketball: my size, strength, and tenacity.

I drew really dark, depressing scenes. Somebody was always crying in my pictures. The main character, who was always a version of me, would be sitting under a tree, her back against the trunk, with crows circling and rain pouring down from a black sky. I would use a red pen to show the tears coming out of her eyes. I wrote stories about kids getting picked on and then beating up the bullies. There was a lot of fighting in my stories, and they never had happy endings. Once I wrote about a girl who cut her wrists and died. I would sometimes imagine what would happen if I did something like that, if I didn't exist anymore. In those moments, I pictured how sad my family would be, how much suffering it would cause my mother. I know now that a lot of kids have similar thoughts, when they think no one understands their pain and that life won't ever get better. I know now how important it is to acknowledge those thoughts and to share them with others. I know now that no matter how much you're hurting, you're not alone, because other people have been in your shoes. Because I've been there myself.

I think I was hoping if I put the pain down on paper, tried to capture what I was feeling, I could find some answers in the process. Not that I was consciously aware of this at the time; it simply felt like what I wanted to do, what I needed to do. Now I see it as a form of therapy. I think kids have an amazing capacity to try and heal themselves, to find whatever outlets they can to express the emotions inside them. When I look back at my twelve-year-old self, I can see I was searching for some kind of release, for a way to break the cycle, even as I continued to act out at school. My world had become so small, it felt like I had nothing to lose.

I would soon learn how wrong I was.

AS IF I DIDN'T HAVE enough to worry about, my life was briefly interrupted the summer after sixth grade, when my parents decided to move. My dad wanted to get out of the city, so we packed up and headed to a house in the country, in a town called Dayton, about forty-five minutes outside Houston. We barely stayed six months, and the whole time we were there, it felt like we were in a constant state of transition. My sister Pier was a senior by then, and she drove back and forth each day to Houston so she could finish high school with her friends. Meanwhile, I missed my old school, which should tell you something about how things were going for me. I was used to the social dynamics of a city school; I knew what to expect every day in Houston. I knew when I had to watch my back, and when I could let down my guard. But in Dayton, I didn't know anybody. I was an outsider, a loner, and I retreated even further into myself.

I liked the idea of being in the country. I had a go-kart and a dune buggy, and a few acres of land to ride around. But when you're in seventh grade and school is miserable, your whole life is miserable. I was skipping classes, mouthing off to teachers, getting bad progress reports. I was a bloody mess—literally. One day during gym class, we were running outside, doing this little cross-country course through the trees, and I turned my head for a second and somehow managed to smack right into a big old oak tree. I roughed up the right side of my face pretty bad and got blood all over my shirt. I was sent to the school nurse's office, but she just told me to wash myself off, so I did. Needless to say, when I got home and my parents got a look at me, they were none too pleased with how things were handled.

Turns out, I wasn't the only one struggling. My mom wasn't happy living there either. She felt isolated, and she was worried about me. She saw a snake in the front yard one day, not long after I had run into the tree at school, and that was the final straw for her. She said to my dad, "I'm sorry, but I'm not a little country woman." It was time to go. So in the middle of the school year, we moved back to Houston, into a two-story house in the Memorial Hills neighborhood, and I enrolled at Teague Middle School. I was happy to leave Dayton, but I also felt like I couldn't get my footing anywhere. I was just thrashing my way through one school to the next, always trying to assert myself as tough.

In eighth grade, I ended up in another bad spot—except this time there was actually a punishment that resonated with me. The seeds were sown when a certain girl started talking nasty to me and some of my friends late that fall. She was always trying to stir up trouble, spreading rumors, running off at the mouth, calling people sluts or dykes, saying crap about their families. She was just real messy. She would nudge me in the hallway, bump me with a shoulder or elbow, clip my heels. And I started doing the same thing, brushing by her to show I wasn't afraid. This went on for weeks, the two of us nudging each other whenever we crossed paths, and it felt like it would continue for the rest of the year unless I put a stop to it. I wanted to make it clear she had picked the wrong enemy, so I sent her a message through one of my friends: "Let's settle this now. Meet me in the bathroom tomorrow during lunch."

The next day, I showed up in the bathroom with a friend. A minute later, Messy Girl arrived with a whole entourage. (I remember her name, but there's no reason to share it.) There were at least eight or nine girls with her. I think they planned to jump me. I was about five foot ten by that point, although it's hard to remember for sure because I was always growing. I was definitely big enough to put her in her place, but not big enough to take on a group of girls all at once. So before anything could happen, I went after her and hit her. She started swinging and scratching, and she ripped my shirt right down the middle. It was hanging off me, like I had been attacked by a tiger. I was furious, enraged. I threw a bunch of punches, connecting pretty good with a couple of them, then got her in a headlock. That's when my friend jumped between us and broke it up, saying we had to get out of there before we got caught. A few seconds later, everyone was running out of the bathroom. I stayed behind because I needed to fix my shirt somehow, or wait there until my friend could go grab one out of the gym bag in my locker. But when Messy Girl had left the bathroom, she went straight to the principal's office and tried to pin the whole thing on me. (All it took was one look at my shirt to see we were both in the wrong.) I didn't even make it out of the bathroom before a school supervisor came to collect me. My dad had to pick me up and take me home. I was suspended from school for three days, but the punishment at home lasted almost two months. I lost what few privileges I had. I couldn't use my TV, and I couldn't leave my room except to eat, shower, and go to the bathroom.

If I'm honest with myself, I know none of those restrictions would have solved the turmoil inside me. But what did, what made me take a long look at my behavior, was that I lost the chance to play basketball because of fighting. I had just tried out for the eighth-grade team with some of my friends, and I had made the squad even though I'd never actually played the sport, beyond goofing around during open gym sessions. Now here I was getting kicked off the team before I could play my first game—which meant another winter of staring at the walls inside my room, hunkered down with my spiral notebook.

ALL THE DRAWINGS and stories I created were meant for my eyes only. Once I finished a picture, I would find a way to destroy it, but first I would usually hide it in my room. I'd fold it up dozens of times until it was no bigger than a quarter, then stuff it somewhere no one would find it. Sometimes I would take a pen and scribble furiously over the paper so you couldn't make out the words or figures; all you could see was an angry streak of black or red. Later, when the trash was going out, I would sneak the folded-up notepaper into the bag just before it was dumped into the garbage truck. I even buried a few letters in our backyard. I put them in a homemade time capsule, so I could read them in the future. But I'm so impatient, I dug them up a week later.

This secret world existed for me only inside my room. When I stepped through the door and rejoined my family, I pretended everything was fine and cool. I was really good at hiding my pain, putting on a brave face, carrying myself with a swagger. It's possible my mom found one or two of my notes, but as far as I know, I kept it all out of sight. I didn't want anyone to know how much I was struggling. I couldn't bear the thought of my parents finding out what kids were saying to me at school, because my mom would get sad and my dad would get mad. I could picture him showing up and chewing out the principal, and I knew that wouldn't change a thing. I realize now how foolish my thinking was, but I felt embarrassed and ashamed.

Writing is still my outlet today. Like everybody, I still struggle to manage certain parts of my life, especially the public version of myself that has to be happy and "on" all the time. Don't get me wrong: I have a lot of things to be happy about. But even if I'm having a bad day or I'm just plain tired, I always try to smile and seem cheerful in public, because you never know who is meeting you or seeing you for the first time. When I get home at night, I might pull open my laptop and write about my day, sprinkling in whatever questions pop into my head. If I'm upset or disappointed about something, I'll write through the scene, what actually happened and how I really feel about it, acknowledging my struggles—all the stuff that is hard to share sometimes, because when people ask you how things are going, the stock answer is "Doin' good!" Nobody wants to hear, "Well, actually . . ."

I've always been a people pleaser, so I try to go along with things in the moment, sometimes saying yes even though I might later regret it, like scheduling appearances on a day off, when all I want to do is rest and chill. Or when someone asks how I'm feeling, I just gloss over it. For example, when my mom calls to check in, I usually tell her I'm good, everything is good. She has enough to worry about with her health; I don't want to drag her down with whatever is bothering me, the little annoyances we all have to deal with in our daily lives. Writing helps me sort through my emotions. And I'm trying to save what I write these days, so I can look back on it later. I'm not trashing my files the way I used to toss my folded-up notepaper in the garbage. But every once in a while, I will delete something I've written, if I don't like the idea of it existing on my computer.

You know what they say: old habits die hard.

38

THE NEW ME

We had a computer in our living room, an eMachine, and I spent a lot of time on it in sixth and seventh grades. My dad was usually at work, sometimes taking extra shifts on nights or weekends, and my mom was good about leaving me alone, not hovering over me. I was thankful for that, because my dad's paranoia felt suffocating. When I knew I had a chunk of time to myself, I would go to the living room and hop on the computer. I still remember the password, or at least most of it: "Morgue" and then a few numbers. (My dad's side of the family ran a funeral home when he was younger.) I would load the Yahoo search page, type in the words *gay and lesbian,* or some combination of the two, then read articles and watch documentaries for hours.

Kids tossed those words around a lot at school, along with *fag* and *dyke* and other slurs, sometimes hurling them as insults at specific targets, like me, and other times casually dropping them into conversation the same way they might use the word *loser*—with friends saying to each other, "That is so gay." When I was twelve, I had a vague idea of what *gay* and *lesbian* meant, but I didn't have any larger context for those words. I just knew that when I heard them, I felt something inside me, a curiosity that made me want to learn more. (Luckily my dad's truck was really loud, so I would hear it rumbling down the street, giving me a two-minute warning. I would immediately clear my search history and log off the computer.)

I knew, from the first afternoon I spent reading about the LGBT community, I was reading about myself, that there were many other people out there like me. I was not alone, and the knowledge of that soothed some of my pain. I had never wanted to dress and act like a lot of the other girls, but I didn't want to be a boy, either. I just did whatever felt natural, without giving it much thought. And when I got on that eMachine, I discovered a whole world of people who felt the same way I did, who lived somewhere in the middle. I learned there are women who identify as "stud" or "butch" lesbians, which generally means they see themselves as occupying a more traditionally masculine role, both in society and in their relationships. Much of how I was feeling internally could be displayed outwardly by my clothes, my gestures, my attitude. I remember sitting at the computer and letting out a long sigh of relief, because I knew someday I would be able to become a complete person, with who I am on the inside matching how I expressed myself on the outside.

Of course, knowing I was gay wasn't the same thing as telling other people I was gay. I didn't feel ready to fully embrace everything I was learning. When I was in middle school, the control that my dad had over my life was ironclad. I knew there was zero chance he would accept me as gay, or let me leave the house dressed in a style that he would see as completely ridiculous. I knew he would (and he later did) say that my sexuality and appearance were a result of being influenced by others. And I wasn't ready to engage in that battle with him. I was already getting picked on for being different, for looking like a boy, for having a low voice, so it was hard to imagine myself doing anything to announce that I was even more different than everyone else already thought. Also, around this time, another girl in seventh grade had come out as a lesbian, or someone had outed her, and the kids were merciless. "Stay away from her," they'd say. "You don't watch to catch the Gay!" It was like she was the boogeyman, ready to pounce at any second.

So I kept all this knowledge—the truth—to myself. That didn't stop kids from whispering behind my back, but I was still pretending I was straight, that I was into boys. I even kissed a boy in seventh grade and acted like we were a couple; that's how desperate I was to prove to everyone else, and maybe even to myself, that maybe I wasn't as different as they thought. Part of why these middle-school years were so hard is because I didn't even have myself to lean on. Kids at school were rejecting me, and in turn I was rejecting my true self, trying different versions of me on for size, to see what I could make fit. It was like each day was an exercise in erasing myself just a little bit more.

I still remember one particular interaction like it happened yesterday, because it's such a clear example of how I was acting at the time. It was the first day of volleyball tryouts in seventh grade (we were living back in Houston), and a bunch of us girls were sitting in the bleachers, waiting for the coach. I kept tugging at my outfit, trying to stretch it out. We had to wear these little form-fitting shirts, cropped in a way that they showed our stomachs if we lifted our arms in the air, which was obviously something we did a lot while playing volleyball. And the shorts were so tiny, they felt like glorified underwear. I was sitting next to my friend Ashton, who lived in the same neighborhood as me. My arms and legs were mostly bare, and I kept rearranging myself because I felt so exposed, so uncomfortable. Sitting in the row in front of us was this girl named Kim, who was part of the in-crowd. She was with her friends, and they were whispering. A minute or two later, Kim turned back to me and said, out of nowhere, "Brittney, you're gay, right?" She said it like she expected my answer to be yes, like she just wanted confirmation of a truth. I didn't really stop to process what she was asking, and before I could, I heard myself answering, almost reflexively, "Yeah."

Kim just nodded and turned back around, kept talking with her friends. All of a sudden I realized what had happened, and I started panicking. I said, "Wait, wait—what? What did you ask me?" She turned around and asked me again, and I made my voice nice and level, like there was no way I could be lying, and told her, "Nah, no, I'm not. Hell no, I'm not." She just kind of shrugged and said, "Okay."

I was determined to fix the situation, so I moved forward into her row, but before I could say anything else, she looked at me and said, "You can scoot back with your friend. We were just asking."

"I'm good," I said, trying to be smooth. "I'm just chilling."

"Whatever," she said, then turned her body away from me and kept talking with her friends.

A minute later, I moved back to my row.

It seems like an odd thing to say, but being who you are can take practice, especially when who you are doesn't fit neatly into the vision that society has for how you should act, what you should wear, who you should love. I haven't always embraced the parts of me that are different, because when you're young, it's scary to voluntarily step away from the mainstream. But I eventually realized that faking it is draining, and that the more people who raise their hands and say, "This is me," the more they help empower other people to do the same.

I decided that at the start of my freshman year of high school, I would stop pretending. I highlighted this date the way many kids point to college as their chance to reinvent themselves. I saw high school as a step into adulthood, when my dad would have less control over me, and I wanted to take that step forward as my true, authentic self. So when ninth grade rolled around, I was ready for it in more ways than one. I started dressing and acting exactly how I wanted to—even if I cringe a little now when I think about how over the top I was in going about it.

I DIDN'T ACTUALLY have my own style back then. I was just copying certain looks I saw on other people, clothes and images that resonated as similar to the "me" I wanted to express. Over the next several years, my style would morph from "rapper boy" to "athletic" to "preppy" to where I am now, a mesh of all those things, a combination that feels right to me. But my first step was to stop wearing ambiguous clothing, those shirts and jeans that still had even a slightly "girly" edge. I felt like an imposter in those clothes. So the first style I truly embraced was loosely defined: all that mattered was feeling comfortable. My go-to outfit was an oversized T-shirt or hoodie with a pair of baggy RocaWear jeans. Even when I went to Baylor, the first year or two, I didn't know precisely what I wanted my style to be. I was all over the place. I would wear our team-issued Nike gear or a pair of Levi's with a polo shirt, or something that reflected my new passion for skateboarding. The "California swag" was strong back then, the Jerky Boy look. So I wore the flannel shirts with colorful skinny jeans and a pair of Vans. I also liked to cut the sleeves off my shirts and throw

43

on some shorts or sweats—my "athletic and lazy" look. (I must admit, I've adopted that look in Phoenix a lot of days, because it's so damn hot in the summer. The less clothing, the better.)

My senior year at Baylor, and especially my rookie year in the WNBA, is when I started paying closer attention to fashion and how I wanted to represent myself away from the court. After trying different styles over the years, I finally realized I could blend them together to create a look unique to me, putting my own spin on the trends. And a key part of my style now has nothing to do with clothes. Since my senior year of high school, I've added one or two tattoos a year. I'm working toward full sleeves on both arms, and I'll probably get more ink on my back. I understand there are people out there who are put off by tattoos. Ink isn't for everyone. There are many different ways to express yourself; it just so happens a lot of people enjoy doing that with tats. We see it as a kind of art, and I don't think we should be judged for it, as if we're doing something rebellious and don't want to follow the rules.

MY FIRST WEEK of ninth grade, I saw that girl Kim in the hallway, the one who had asked me if I was gay when we were in seventh grade. She looked me up and down—I was wearing a big hoodie, sagging my jeans—and said, "Oh, okay." She wasn't mean about it; her tone was more like, "I knew it." I'm pretty sure she was thinking back to that moment at volleyball tryouts two years earlier, when I went out of my way to deny who I was. So standing there in the hallway, I just looked her in the eyes and said, "Yeah, you know, shit happens." That's exactly what I said. Then I shrugged and kept walking.

I laugh when I think about it now, because "shit happens" sounds like a terrible way to acknowledge your sexual identity. But I was actually feeling pretty good about myself. It was obvious by the way I was dressing that I was trying to make a statement. And when kids asked me if I was gay, I would say, "Yup." Word spread pretty quickly in high school, so I didn't really have to tell a lot of people myself. It just became common knowledge. The fact that I was six feet tall by then and playing volleyball helped me avoid some of the name-calling I had endured in middle school. Not all of it—sometimes when I walked into the gym, guys would say stuff like, "Yo, you can untuck now!"—but as I would quickly discover, being an athlete carried some status with the cool crowd. And the more my self-confidence grew, the less I worried about what other people were saying.

Don't get me wrong: it's not like all the lights switched on for me at once, magically, with a choir singing in the background and everyone in my life embracing me for who I was trying to become. It was a big, long process, and I had my share of missteps and detours. Telling my father I was gay just wasn't an option at that point. But telling my mother felt like a necessity, an instinctive urge to share my truth, because I trusted her so much, and I think I knew, deep down, I would need her love and support for the journey ahead. So one afternoon during my freshman year, I came right out and told her. I was leaning against the wall in our kitchen, and I just said the words, "Mom, I'm gay." I hadn't even planned the moment; it just felt right. She smiled, hugged me, and told me she loved me. That was it.

I know now that a lot of kids aren't as fortunate as I was, to have a moment like that, to have at least one parent they can confide in and lean on when they're trying to figure out who they are. And believe me, I still had a lot to figure out. When I look back at my fifteen-year-old self, I can't help but shake my head. I remember walking down the hallways at school, with my jeans sagging, my boxer shorts showing, using really hard-core hand gestures, my voice all rough and edgy. I was going overboard with my new look,

45

which tends to happen when you've felt restrained for so long: you end up snapping to the other end of the spectrum, like an elastic being released. But when I came home from school, and I was walking those final steps before I got to the back door of our house, I would yank up my jeans and tighten my belt, reminding myself to tone down my mannerisms.

Being true to myself has often been at odds with my desire to please others. I've spent years trying so hard to be the version of myself that would make the most people happy. Over time, though, I've come to realize that no matter how much I compromise, some people will never understand me. And accepting this truth has given me a new level of comfort and freedom.

HOOKED ON HOOPS

On game days, I like getting to the arena early, so I have plenty of time to go through my pregame routine and get focused, settle down, clear my head of everything else. I sit and listen to music for a while; then I go around and say hi to my teammates as they start to roll in. Whenever I can, I try to hit the court and work on my post moves before practice or pregame warm-ups. I got a late start with basketball, so I feel like I'm always learning. People say, "You can't teach height," and obviously my height gives me some advantages as a player. But height only takes you so far, especially in the WNBA, where I'm routinely going up against big, strong, powerful women with more experience as pros. I got into foul trouble early during my first game in the league, when we got blown out by Chicago. I kept leaving my feet and trying to block every shot in sight, even though I know better than that. I'm already six foot eight, so there's no need to make myself taller. I played smarter in the second half, once I had a chance to collect myself, but I was so amped up in that first half, it was like I was back in ninth grade, running up and down the court without a clue.

I started playing soccer and volleyball when I was in seventh grade. I tried out for the school teams with some of my friends, mostly because sports were the only activity my dad allowed me to do—the only time I could hang out with other kids and feel like I was part of the group. I had always been full of energy when I was little, constantly in motion, and I quickly came to love the competitiveness and intensity of sports. Volleyball was fun because I got to spike and block; hitting that ball, or rising up to deny someone, felt so good. I played goalkeeper in soccer because I liked to use my hands (and because I didn't want to run around much). Everybody focuses on scoring in sports—that's where most of the glory is—but I liked being the one to stop people from scoring.

48

Starting in seventh grade, I would hang out with kids in the gym sometimes before school and mess around with the basketball, but I didn't know what I was doing and I never practiced on my own. It wasn't until eighth grade, when some of my friends tried out for the team, that I decided to give it a shot. But the start of my hoops career was delayed because of the big fight I got into with Messy Girl in the bathroom. When I told myself everything would be different in ninth grade, that I would stop pretending and start with a clean slate, I had given myself hope, a lifeline to get through middle school. The problem was, I still had to show up every day, see all the same faces, swallow my emotions. I was scared, and I had no idea yet how much basketball would later sustain me. It wasn't until high school that I realized the opportunity I had lost when I got kicked off the team in eighth grade.

By the time I entered ninth grade at Nimitz High School, I

was a solid six feet and eager to write a new story for myself, a real story that I could live in public instead of crumpling up the paper and hiding it somewhere in my bedroom. I played volleyball again that fall, and I caught the eye of the varsity basketball coach, Debbie Jackson, who asked me to try out. My hoop skills were trash. I was clumsy and fumbled the ball a lot—I couldn't dribble more than once or twice without losing it—and I wasn't very strong. But I had decent footwork from playing soccer, and volleyball helped me with my timing, so I was good at blocking shots. Basically, Coach Jackson thought I had a lot of potential. I didn't have much else at that point, just size, potential, and the desire to get better, a good enough combination for me to make the junior varsity, then move up to the varsity after a half-dozen or so games. I averaged around 10 points a game that season, mostly coming off the bench, and I blocked a lot of shots.

I also kept growing. I was about six foot three by the summer after my freshman year, tall enough to attract attention from recruiters. Up until then, the idea of going to college had never really crossed my mind. Whenever I imagined my future, I always saw myself graduating from high school and becoming a cop. Neither of my parents had attended college—my dad joined the military, and my mom took some secretarial classes at a small business school—so it wasn't something on my radar. That summer, though, I started getting letters from colleges, which is when I finally realized what Coach Jackson and other people meant when they told me I had potential. It wasn't just about how good I could be at basketball; it was about the doors that basketball could open for me. I was playing AAU (Amateur Athletic Union) ball for the Houston Hotshots, which exposed me to a lot of good local competition, and all I had to do was look around me to see examples of how I could improve my game.

The growing confidence I felt off the court carried over to

basketball. And the more I improved as a player, the better I felt about the person I was becoming. It all just fed on itself. After fighting and struggling my way through middle school, I now had a new sense of purpose. Basketball became another form of expression for me, and when my sophomore season rolled around, I was ready to express myself loudly. My skills were still raw, but the game was starting to click for me, and the competitive outlet became even more important because I had given up volleyball after ninth grade. I wish I could say I quit volleyball to focus my energy on hoops, but the truth is, my decision was mainly a fashion choice. I just couldn't wear those tight shorts anymore. I had asked the coach if I could wear basketball shorts, and she said no. So then I suggested track shorts, which were closer in length to our volleyball shorts but looser and less constricting—you know, not all up on my ass. Coach said no again. So that was the end of my volleyball career. I spent all of middle school feeling uncomfortable in my own skin; there was no way I was going to spend another minute wearing anything I didn't want to wear.

The funny thing is, the first time I ever dunked was during volleyball practice. It was my freshman year, and there was a guy who worked with us sometimes, a school employee, and one day he tossed me a volleyball and said, "Brittney, go dunk that." I hesitated and gave him a look that said, "Do what?" So he said it again. "Go dunk that ball. I want to see if you can do it." I had watched guys throw down in the gym before, but it wasn't something I had thought about trying myself. I could barely dribble at the time. I walked to the top of the key, took a few running steps, raised the volleyball over my head, and plunked it through the net as my fingers grazed off the rim. It wasn't much of a dunk, but I got it down. And just like that, I was hooked. I became as obsessed with dunking as everyone else. I wanted to get better at it, and I practiced with the guys during open gym sessions that winter, trying to get the timing and coordination right. I also became serious about working out, which helped my jumping ability.

The first time I dunked a basketball was during my sophomore season with the girls' varsity. We were scrimmaging one day, and somebody got a steal and threw the ball ahead to me. I had some space, so I took a couple of steps, jumped up, and dunked it one-handed, like it was no big deal. Everyone was like, "Girl, you just dunked that!" And then they wanted me do it again, just to be sure. So I did. You could feel the energy level rise in the gym. That's what I love about dunking: it's like turning the volume way up on a good song. It's a powerful thing. In fact, the first time I dunked in a game, later that season, it felt like the whole gym was on full blast. We were winning big, and I got the ball on a fast break, so I put an exclamation point on things and slammed it home. Everybody went nuts. My teammates were jumping on me, the fans were falling all over themselves in the stands. Coach Jackson had to call a time-out just to settle us down.

It's not every day you see a sixteen-year-old girl dunk. And I could dunk easily. In January 2007, during my sophomore season, somebody made a video of me—*High School Girl Dunker*—and uploaded it on YouTube. It went viral, and that's when the media really started paying attention. Obviously, it helped that I could do more than just dunk. I averaged 22 points and almost 11 rebounds and 6 blocks a game that season. And by the end of the spring, I had grown to six foot six.

I was feeling pretty good about my body. I was getting stronger, and being an athlete gave me a sense of focus. It's crazy: the same thing that got me picked on in middle school—my body—was now a plus for me, just because I played basketball. So I wasn't, like, "Oh my God, I wish I would stop growing!" I was okay with it, especially because I wasn't in physical pain anymore. All throughout the seventh and eighth grades, I had tremendous pains. My knees ached so badly I would cry. Even if I just lightly bumped something, I would feel a sharp jolt that put me in tears. Meanwhile, I had no idea it was growing pains. Pretty ironic, right? With all the other crap that was happening in middle school, all the emotional agony, here I was in physical pain, too. My dad actually took me to the doctor in eighth grade to have everything checked out, to see why I was growing so quickly and make sure I didn't have any kind of disease or a tumor pressing on my pituitary gland. They did all sorts of tests, and everything was fine. My growth plates were just wide open. The doctor said, "Yeah, she's going to grow a lot." My dad is six two and my mom is five eight, and the doctor predicted I'd be around six three. (Wrong!) The funny thing is, the pain in my knees stopped when I got to ninth grade, but that's when I really shot up fast.

THE SUMMER AFTER my sophomore year, I switched AAU teams and played for DFW Elite in Dallas. The Hotshots didn't really travel outside Houston, and I wanted tougher competition. DFW Elite was sponsored by Nike and was one of the top AAU teams in the country, so we went to all the major events, like the Nike National Invitational Tournament in Chicago. A bunch of my future Baylor teammates played on that squad: Odyssey Sims, Brooklyn Pope, Jordan Madden, Kimetria Hayden, and Makenzie Robertson. Anyone who knows anything about women's college hoops knows that Makenzie is Kim Mulkey's daughter. So you can imagine all the buzz that created, with people saying Kim had an unfair recruiting advantage. I didn't know much about the recruiting process and how it all worked, but I had seen and heard enough to know I wanted to avoid all the craziness you read about—the phone calls and texts from lots of schools, the pressure of weighing the pros and cons of different programs, the campus visits, the media speculation. I had enough drama in my life already. The last thing I needed was a parade of coaches in my head.

"BIG GIRL IS COMING TO BAYLOR!"

If I hadn't gone to Baylor, I probably would have chosen Texas A&M or maybe Tennessee. But that's all hypothetical, because the truth is that I only had eyes for Baylor. Once I really started paying attention to colleges, during my sophomore season at Nimitz, I began to realize how many things about Baylor I liked. One of my good friends on the Houston Hotshots, Kelli Griffin, had decided to play there. She was two years ahead of me, so I already knew a little bit about the school. The location was perfect for me; Waco is only three hours from Houston, and I liked the small-town feel of it and the compact size of the campus. I knew Baylor assistant coach Damion McKinney because he had previously been involved with my AAU program in Dallas, DFW Elite. He's an awesome dude, and I felt really comfortable around him. I liked Kim, too. I had a decent sense of her personality just from being around Makenzie with the AAU squad and watching the two of them interact. I saw some of the same traits in Kim that I saw in my dad—they're both intense, tough-talking authority types—and even though I resented how strict, how overwhelming, my dad could be, I was also used to putting up with it. And from what I could tell, Kim seemed more fair and understanding. I was so sheltered and contained, I knew that when I got to college I would probably let loose, and I needed a coach who would let me get my wild out while still being able to keep me in line.

I attended Baylor's camp during the summer after my sophomore year of high school. Until then, I had actually spent more time in College Station, watching Texas A&M. I went to a bunch of Aggies games during the winter, because the school was only ninety minutes from Houston. I think their coach, Gary Blair, thought I was destined to choose A&M. But I fell in love with Baylor at that summer camp. The campus was just small enough that I could walk everywhere I needed to go; it wasn't huge and sprawling like the University of Texas in Austin. I also liked the vibe I got when I talked to Kim in between sessions. I would seek her out on my way to get water and ask her questions about the drills we were doing. I was a sponge, because basketball still felt so new to me.

On the last day of camp, we were scrimmaging, and I was going hard, wanting to prove myself. The Baylor players, who were working the camp, were watching from the sidelines, and they were pumping me up, shouting encouragement. At one point in the middle of playing, I thought to myself, *Damn, I like it here. I'm going to commit.* As soon as the drill ended, I jogged over to my dad, who was watching in the stands, and I said to him, "I want to commit here. What do you think about that?" I figured he would be happy about it, because it meant I would stay in state, so he could still see me play and keep an eye on me. Even though our relationship was growing more strained, I still recognized and appreciated all the ways in which he supported my budding basketball career.

MY DAD DROVE ME everywhere for hoops, partly because he didn't like me going anywhere alone. We spent countless hours together in his truck, driving to and from AAU practice, to and from tournaments. I remember one day, his boss didn't want to give him the time off he was requesting, and I overheard Dad say into the phone, "Well, my girl has a tournament and I'm going to be there. You can fire me if you want." He didn't know I could hear him, but it made me happy. He never missed a game. Throughout my college career, he would always drive to Waco and back in one night, even if he had to be at work by six o'clock the next morning. I call him the Protector. Some of my AAU teammates would hop rides with other people's moms, making long road trips in a van that usually had a cooler filled with Gatorades and snacks. But not me. Nope. No way. My dad and I would ride together in his truck, to South Carolina or Alabama. If he didn't go, I didn't go. But he always went. And those rides were actually pretty cool. We would just talk about random stuff, nothing heavy, but I was glad to have any connection with my dad, even if it was superficial. Without basketball, we probably wouldn't have spent time together during my teenage years.

I could also always count on my dad to be stoic during my games. He wasn't one of those parents who become emotional when their kids play, or yell at the coach, or call out instructions. He would just sit on the sideline, no emotion, even if it was the final play of a close game and everyone else was standing up and screaming. He saved his criticisms and advice for after the game, but I never felt compelled to listen too closely because he had never played basketball. In fact, he only started watching it the year I started playing it. Of course, that didn't keep him from offering advice about what I could do better. But he stopped doing it once I got to college, because he knew it bothered me. He would just say something simple and positive, like "Good game" or "You played well." Occasionally, he would even say, "I'm proud of you." He did that more often when I was at Baylor, and it felt good to hear.

My dad is an extremely private man. He frowns upon people calling attention to themselves, even in situations meant to publicly honor them. I remember at my sister Pier's graduation, in the moments before her name was called, he turned to the rest of us, me and DeCarlo and SheKera, and said, "Don't jump up. Don't y'all be loud." We rolled our eyes at him and looked at each other like, *Um, okay!* The instant Pier's name was called over the loudspeaker, we jumped out of our seats, screaming with excitement. Everyone turned and looked at us, because we were going crazy.

56   That's especially what my dad hates: the spotlight. When I first started getting media attention in high school because of my dunking, he would say to me, practically growling, "I ain't gonna be interviewed, am I?" Over time, obviously, he did have to deal with reporters. And if somebody asked him a question, he would fall back on his experience as a police officer. You know how when something bad happens, and the cops hold a press briefing? Well, he had to do those on occasion, and he'd stand there in uniform, looking all stoic and tough, giving the shortest, most stripped-down answers. And that's how he handled interviews about me, too.

WHEN I JOGGED OVER to my dad at the Baylor summer camp, I wanted his approval—I still do, to this day—because he had already put so much time into my basketball activities. So I told him I wanted to commit to Baylor and asked him what he thought. "I don't have a problem with that," he said. And that was it. I smiled, then jogged away to finish the last few hours of camp. I knew from some of my friends, like Kelli, that you can't commit to a college while you're attending summer camp there; the NCAA has a rule against it, intended to protect kids from making impulsive decisions and to keep the camps from turning into recruiting circuses. I get the idea behind it, but the way it played out for me was pretty comical. The rule requires that a recruit must leave school grounds before committing. So when camp was over, I asked Kim if she was going to stick around for a while, because I planned to come right back. She said yes, she would be in her office. Then my dad and I left the Ferrell Center, got into his truck, drove off campus, made a U-turn, and headed straight back to the arena. We also called my mom to let her know what was happening, and she was so excited that I had decided to stay close to home.

The women's basketball offices overlook the practice court, which is attached to the Ferrell Center. There is a reception area right when you walk in, then a long hallway lined with pictures and awards. Kim's office is in the back corner. I remember looking at all the pictures as I walked toward her office. There was a celebration shot from the 2005 NCAA championship game, after Baylor had won, and I said to myself, *Oh my God, I want to do that. I want to win one of those.* I was nodding my head, looking at all the action shots, and thinking, *Yeah, I can see myself in green and gold.*

When we got to Kim's office, all the coaches were there, along with a few players. My dad and I sat next to each other, across from Kim, who was at her desk. Someone handed me a Barq's root beer. I remember that distinctly because root beer is my favorite soda, and it felt like a sign to me that they had root beer in the fridge. On the wall over Kim's shoulder was a glass case containing all the championship rings she had won, from USA basketball, Baylor, her playing days at Louisiana Tech. I looked

57

at them and decided I wanted to win them for myself, too. I was fidgeting in my seat, because I didn't know the exact words to say.

"So, Coach," I began, "I don't know how this goes. I don't know what to say. But I want to come here. Do you want me?"

She smiled and said, "Big Girl, of course I do!" Then she got serious for a moment. "You realize you're making a verbal commitment and you have to go by your word?"

"Yeah," I said. "I mean, yes, ma'am. I understand." I had a confused look on my face, because I thought that's exactly what I was doing, making a verbal commitment. So I said it again, with conviction. "Yes. I want to come to Baylor."

When Kim heard that, she started shouting—"Big Girl is coming to Baylor!"—and the door burst open and people poured in. They must have been waiting just outside, with their ears pinned to the door. It was like they were spilling out of a clown car. Damion was pumping his fist and hollering, "Yeah, yeah, yeah, Big Girl is here!" And Rekha Patterson, another assistant coach, was whooping it up at the top of her lungs. Then we all had a big group hug, like family, right inside Kim's office. They were all so excited, like I was a big deal, and their reaction made me feel good, important. I mean, I knew I was a high-level recruit, because I was listed in all the rankings as one of the best players in the country. But I had been hooping for only a couple of years, and I wasn't that far removed from the confused middle-school kid who figured she would join the military after high school. I didn't have years of AAU ball—some kids start playing at age nine or ten—to build my ego. So that moment in Kim's office meant so much to me.

Even though a verbal commitment isn't legally binding, most teams stopped calling me once word got out that I had said yes to Baylor. Schools still expressed their interest, but the only coach who seriously hung around—I guess in case I changed my mind for some reason—was Gary Blair at Texas A&M. He showed up at a lot of my high school games, and he kept recruiting me until the day I signed on the dotted line with Baylor, November 12, 2008, in my senior year of high school. I have to give him credit.

Some kids might get a rush from all the attention that comes with the recruiting game, but I was happy to avoid most of it. I have friends who didn't decide on their schools until the last minute, and by the end of it all, they were sick of the whole process. They were sick of hearing the phone ring and feeling obligated to talk. And I'm sure a lot of coaches get tired of chasing after players. It's just one big song and dance, with everyone playing a role. Kim had to walk a fine line as a mother and as a coach, because Makenzie played on the same AAU team with girls who were being recruited by Baylor. I know there are plenty of folks who think Kim took advantage of the situation, but I think that's just sour grapes. It's not like Kim gave birth to Makenzie in the hopes that she would eventually grow up to play basketball at the same time, on the same AAU team, as one of the top recruits in the country. All coaches walk the line, trying to get every advantage they can while staying within the rules (or not getting caught breaking the rules). Everyone is looking for an edge.

A week after we won the national championship at Baylor, during my junior season, the NCAA put our program on probation for three years, along with the men's basketball team, after the school reported itself for rules violations, because various members of the coaching staffs had made "impermissible" phone calls and sent too many text messages to recruits—more than the rules allowed. In my case specifically, it was a minor violation for the coaches to talk about the Baylor program, in any way, when I attended that summer camp, even though I had asked them questions. It was also a violation for Kim to sit next to my dad during AAU games and talk about life as a Baylor athlete, even after I

59

had verbally committed to the school. I could easily launch into a big long tangent here about the business of college sports, and the NCAA, and the hypocrisy and controversy around all of it, but that's not really my battle. I have other issues and causes that are closer to my heart. Let's just say I can't even imagine what a circus my life would have been like if I hadn't picked a college early on, if I had waited for other schools to roll out the red carpet and recruit me hard. No thank you.

I will admit, though, I did enjoy the ego boost I got when the recruiting letters first started coming after ninth grade. I was reminded of that a few weeks into my rookie season in Phoenix. My mom called me one day when she was doing some spring cleaning and came across a box of recruiting letters I had saved. She asked me, "Do you still want these?" And I didn't even hesitate. "Yes!" I said. "Do not throw away my letters!" I'm sure at some point I won't care anymore, but right now I still see that box of letters as a reminder of how my life went in a different direction, and how I'm trying to make the most of this opportunity.

60

RAY FINDS OUT

I love my dad so much. When I close my eyes, I can see myself as a little girl, following him everywhere. I wanted to be just like him. And I hold tight to the good memories now—us fixing cars together, watching military shows, me looking through an old trunk filled with his letters from Vietnam—because so much has changed between us. I know I can't let myself forget how close we were. I can't let myself forget that I was once a daddy's girl. But as I've grown older, I've come to realize my father is not an easy man. Maybe the problem is we're too much alike. It's almost as if we're the same puzzle piece, so nothing fits together; we're just always clashing, bumping heads. He is an old-school tough-love disciplinarian, because that's how he was raised.

My dad had a rough upbringing. I mentioned earlier he was

born in Texas. But to be more specific, he was born in Jasper, which was a tough town for blacks in the 1950s and 1960s and still has a lot of racial tension today. (One of the most infamous hate crimes in U.S. history happened there, in 1998, when James Byrd Jr., an African American, was chained to a pickup truck by three white men and dragged to his death.) My dad spent the first few years of his life in Jasper, but his mother died when he was real young, from some kind of heart issue, and he was raised by extended family before getting sent off to California in middle school, because he didn't really like his father's second wife. He lived with his aunt and uncle in the Watts section of Los Angeles, and his uncle made him stay in the house or yard all the time, especially after the Watts riots in 1965. My dad was a teenager by then, but whenever he asked if he could go play with friends or walk to the corner store, his uncle would say, "Hell, no. You're staying in the house." He couldn't go anywhere.

Sound familiar?

When I was a kid, my dad still had a lot of family near Jasper, and sometimes I would tag along when he'd visit one of his aunts, who lived in the same house he had once lived in. We'd cut the grass and do some chores, and I loved going up there and exploring. The property had two houses and a barn, but I couldn't go into the house in back, his grandparents' old place, because it was all boarded up. (Dad didn't go near it because he thought there might be snakes.) I would look at that house and sigh. He made it seem like it was filled with treasures: photos, pictures, all kinds of good stuff I wanted to get. But I'll never know, because we usually just cut the grass and drove home. And once Dad's aunt died, we stopped going altogether.

I know it was hard for him, moving from Texas to California as a kid, growing up in a place that never really seemed like home, feeling like he had no freedom. He enlisted in the Marines and

62

served in Vietnam from 1968 to 1969. The way he explained it to me, he wanted to prove he could make it on his own, show his aunt and uncle he could take care of himself. And I always said to him, "You wanted freedom, but you went to the Marines! Of all the places you could go, and that's what you chose?" But he thought it proved how tough he was. He told me stories about wading through the swamps, covered in leeches, walking through the jungle and seeing people get blown up, watching his buddies fall into pits full of bamboo spikes. He even told me about the scar he got near his right eye, from a piece of flying shrapnel. He didn't really talk about that stuff with Mom or my siblings, but I asked him a lot of questions, everything I could think of, and he was good about answering me, telling me what he could remember, sharing more stories as I got older, about the more violent and gruesome things he saw. He also had a trunk with a lot of stuff in it, photos and letters. He let me go through it and read the notes he wrote to his sister, telling her how much he wanted to come home.

SOMETIMES, WHEN I THINK about how my dad rejected me for being gay, I try to remember he grew up at a different time, that he was raised by an older generation with old-fashioned thinking. But then I think about how close we used to be, and I can't help feeling sad, crushed, and frustrated that our relationship is so superficial now. When I was little, I wanted nothing more than to make my dad happy. We were best friends. He put me on a pedestal and made me feel like I was the golden child. I would hear him bragging about me to my mom, to my siblings, to neighbors and friends. And I loved it. I wanted to keep being his go-to baby girl, the one who made him proud because I could change the oil and find the exact tool he wanted. He and Mom would occasionally argue about how much I was doing in the garage and in the yard, hard chores, all his different projects. She didn't want me sliding underneath the car to see the inner workings of it, because she worried about a freak accident. Dad would say to her, "She can do what she wants. It's good she's learning this stuff. She's a little tomboy, is all, and she's helping me out." I loved hearing him defend me like that, like we were on the same team.

Things started changing between us when I was in the seventh and eighth grades. That's when we began drifting apart. Actually, it wasn't drifting so much as actively disagreeing about anything and everything. I was becoming my own person, and I think he liked it better when I was his little girl, absorbing every word he said like it was gospel. I was thinking for myself more, playing soccer and volleyball and trying to make friends, challenging his paranoid assumptions about everyone. There was a bit of a cold war going on between us, but I knew our relationship would become red hot if he discovered the truth about my sexuality. I knew if he found out, the walls would come crashing down around me. My dad has always had a very narrow view of the world, perceiving anything "different" as a threat. He saw bad things every day as a police officer, and his response was to keep me close, right there in the front yard. He wanted to keep me safe, and I knew he wouldn't see being gay as a safe path to travel.

When I told my mother I was gay, we both knew, without having a long discussion about it, that telling my father was out of the question. My mom didn't tell him. I didn't tell him. Whenever I even thought about what might happen if he found out—well, let's just say I quickly pushed that thought out of my mind.

There was no road map for how to handle my dad if he discovered my secret. All bets were off. And I think I started to believe the day would never come. I made it all the way to senior year of high school without him finding out. It wasn't like our relationship was good at that point, anyway. By senior year, I had basically

64

stopped speaking with him, beyond a few meaningless words here and there. When he was home from work, I spent most of my time in my room. I would come out to eat and shower, and that was about it. All my actions around him felt strained.

He obviously suspected I was gay, because he would occasionally say something cryptic or passive-aggressive about my scholarship to Baylor, like "Wonder what Kim is going to think about you being so friendly with gays." Several of my teammates in high school were openly gay, and I knew my dad disliked them. One time, during my junior year, he wondered out loud what would happen if I lost my scholarship. (I hadn't officially signed my letter of intent yet, but everyone knew I was committed to Baylor.) I had already exchanged a few text messages with Kim that day, so after my dad made his comment, I sent her a text and said, "I'm gay. I hope that's not a problem." Kim ended up calling me, and I said it again, on the phone: "I hope it's not a problem, but I'm gay."

I remember she said, "Big Girl, I don't care what you are. You can be black, white, blue, purple, whatever. As long as you come here and do what you need to do and hoop, I don't care." She basically did that whole thing people do when they're trying to seem cool with it but don't really know how to talk about it. (Being gay is a real thing; nobody is blue or purple unless they're choking to death.) But I didn't think there was anything strange about her reaction at the time. I was a high school junior looking for some reassurance, which is what Kim gave me. I felt relieved knowing she supported me, and that my scholarship wasn't in jeopardy.

Of course I was still nervous about my dad. One day after basketball practice, during the middle of my senior season, I walked over to my gym bag and pulled out my phone. I had about twenty missed calls from him, and a text saying, "You need to bring your ass home—now." I also had a missed call from my mom, so I called her back right away. "Your dad knows," she told me. She explained that the mother of a teammate had discovered her daughter was gay, and now this lady knew I was gay, and she called our home to "warn" my parents. Naturally, my dad was the one who answered. After I hung up with my mom, I could feel the panic rising inside me. I packed my gym bag, walked to my car, and drove home.

When I pulled into the driveway, my dad was in the garage. He had just finished cutting the grass. I turned off the ignition, then took a deep breath before stepping out of the car.

"Hey, what's up?" I said, not sure of what else to say. He didn't look up from whatever he was doing, fussing with his tools.

"Come here," he said, sounding pissed, and when I walked into the garage, he glanced over and asked, "Something you need to tell me?"

I still didn't feel compelled to tell him anything, especially in that moment, when he was clearly agitated. Maybe I thought if he wanted to have this conversation with me—if he really wanted to talk about my identity—he needed to do the work.

"No, nothing that I can think of," I said.

"Don't fuck around with me," he said with a cold stare. "Don't be lying to me."

"Just say what you need to say," I answered. "What is it?"

"You're dating girls, ain't you?"

"Yeah, I am."

He kept glaring at me, then went back to doing whatever it was he was doing in the garage, slamming things around. He would make some loud noise, bang a wrench into the toolbox, then look at me sideways. It felt like he was winding himself up for a big fight. I was scared, but stayed right where I was standing. I didn't know what was going to happen.

And then he exploded.

"I ain't raising no gay girl in my house! You can pack your shit and get the fuck out! You're letting these damn dykes influence you to do things you don't even want to do yourself."

I started to respond—"Ain't nobody influencing me"—but he interrupted.

"Don't say nothing," he said. "Don't say shit." And then he stormed off, like a human tornado blowing to some other corner of the garage.

I went into the house and found my mother. "Mom, I can't take this," I told her. "We're going to end up going at it—hard."

I walked upstairs to my room and closed the door. A minute later, my dad came back into the house and yelled up to me, "Come down here!" I knew there was no use ignoring him, so I walked to the top of the stairs and looked down at him.

"So," he said, "this is you?" He was glaring at me again, his voice dripping with disgust. "This is your doing?"

"Yes, this is me," I said. "And it's been me for a while."

I walked down the stairs and started smart-mouthing him. I had so much to say to him after five years of clashing and bumping heads, after so much time feeling like he was ignoring the real me.

"It's been me, and I don't know how you can't know that," I said loudly. "It's so obvious. I know you see my boxers and briefs in the laundry. Who the hell you think it is?"

Before this day, I had never come out and said the words *I'm gay* to my father. But the way I chose to express myself was a pretty good indication. I was wearing baggy jeans and oversized T-shirts and men's sneakers. I also wore boxer shorts, because they're a hell of a lot more comfortable than skimpy little panties. My dad had seen my boxers in the laundry and asked about them, asked who they belonged to, and I had said, "They're mine!" So by this point, it felt like he was ignoring all the signs in front of him—ignoring me—on purpose. It was like he had one picture of who

67

I should be, in his mind, and any time I didn't fit into that vision, he dismissed me. In his eyes, I was an embarrassment, a failure.

By now we were both downstairs, and he just went off again, saying I was being influenced by my "dyke" friends. I walked away from him and went back upstairs, but he followed me, like an angry dog on my heels, just going at me hard, telling me I couldn't use the car anymore, that no girl would ever be allowed in the house again. He kept repeating himself—"I ain't raising no gay-ass girl! You can pack your shit and get the fuck out!"—even though I was clearly trying to end the conversation by walking away.

When I reached my bedroom door, I turned around and shouted, "Look, I don't want to talk! I don't want you to talk to me!"

Then I shut myself in my room. I kept going back and forth in my mind, convincing myself I was tough and independent—I packed my bags and stuffed them underneath my bed, just in case he came into my room—while also crying uncontrollably, acting exactly like a little girl whose daddy had just walked out the door and wasn't coming back. I felt like my heart had been stepped on, like my chest had been crushed. Tears were streaming down my cheeks as I decided what I needed to do next.

Meanwhile, my dad called DeCarlo and SheKera, thinking they would come talk some sense into me. But when they stopped by the house later, they just quietly slipped into my room, sat next to me on the bed, asked if I was okay, gave me a lot of support. They both said, "Get through this year, and then you'll be at Baylor, away from all this."

I cried all night. I think I knew nothing would ever be the same between me and my dad. I thought about throwing my packed bags in the car and just driving: away from him, away from school, away from everything. But I also knew I had a scholarship waiting for me in Waco. If I could just get to Baylor and hoop, then I could make it on my own, without him. So I called Ne'Keisha King, who was the assistant coach for my high school team, and told her everything that was happening, told her I couldn't keep living under the same roof as my dad. She said I could come stay with her while I figured everything out.

At some point during the night, my mom came into my room to check on me. I showed her the bags underneath the bed and told her I was leaving the next day, going to stay with Coach King. She was sitting on the end of my bed and started crying. We were both crying. She didn't want me to go, but she understood why I had to do it.

My dad left for work early the next morning. Despite his threats of taking away the car, a silver Dodge Magnum, he left it in the driveway. I carried my bags downstairs and put them into the car. My mom walked outside with me, and it was one of the saddest moments of my life. It felt like I was going off to war. I honestly didn't know when, or if, I would ever come home. She broke down crying again, until she had no more tears left to cry. Then she gave me some money. DeCarlo came over, too, and slid me some cash. I hugged them both and got into the car.

When I got to Nimitz that morning, I went to see my criminal law teacher. The two of us were close, and I had talked to him throughout the year about how tough things were with my dad. I asked him if he could follow me home later, then give me a lift back to school, so I could leave the Dodge for my dad, because I would be staying with Coach King now. My teacher said yes, sure, anything I needed, and I felt a little better the next few hours. But as I drove back to my neighborhood that afternoon, I began stewing about everything my dad had said, how unfair he was being, how much I hated to hurt my mom by leaving home.

I parked at the clubhouse of our subdivision and called my

69

dad. "You can come get your damn car," I said. "It's at the club-house." And then I just hung up, didn't even wait for his response. Nothing he could say would change my mind. I put my cell phone on the dashboard, so he couldn't contact me, and left the keys in the cup holder. I got out of the car, slammed the door, and rode back to school with my teacher.

A few days later, Pier got me a new phone. My mom had the number, and we talked every day—my brother and sisters, too. Going to school and basketball practice felt the same as before; the difference was that when I got back to Coach King's place, I could relax. I had a peace of mind that didn't exist when I was in the same house as my dad. I could breathe easier, no longer tuned to the sound of his Hummer pulling into the driveway, as I braced for hostile interactions. Unfortunately, that new sense of calm lasted only about three weeks before he got my new cell-phone number. I don't know how he got it, but he did. And he started calling all the time, still saying the same things, that I was letting myself be influenced, that he didn't want no gay-ass daughter. Sometimes I ignored his calls or would hang up as soon as he started in on me. But other times I would fight back, speak my mind, saying some variation of the following: "You don't care about me. You act like I'm a different person, but I'm the same person I've always been. Ain't nobody influencing me; you just don't ever want to hear what I have to say. You say I'm not being myself, but you don't even know who I am. You're my dad, but you don't even know who I am."

None of it mattered. He wouldn't listen. He wouldn't hear me. The only thing that got his attention is when I ignored him completely. A few more weeks went by before he finally decided to change his tune.

"Can we just talk?" he asked when I actually answered one of his calls. "I just want to talk. I don't want to fuss and fight."

He started crying into the phone. But I was so angry and hurt—the walls I had built were thick and high—and I wanted to make him feel the kind of emptiness and pain I had been feeling.

So I hung up on him.

I HAD BEEN LIVING with Coach King for about six weeks when my dad showed up at Nimitz one day and tried to check me out of school. I was in the middle of my senior season, and I was playing better than ever. I've never cared much about stats—if my team is winning a lot of games, I figure I'm doing something right—but when I see the numbers from my senior year, I'm reminded of how far I had come in just a short time. I averaged 33 points, 15.5 rebounds, and 11.7 blocks a game. I actually had 25 blocks in our first game. That was crazy. I also dunked about 50 times that season. Best of all, our team would end up winning a regional championship, and we made it to the state tournament for the first time in school history, losing in the title game. I was on a roll with hoops, despite everything else going on in my life. So the last thing I needed was more drama with my dad. When someone from the main office pulled me out of class and told me he was there, I made it clear I didn't want to see him. "No way," I said. "I'm not going home with him. I'm going back to class."

I had actually just seen him a few days before, on Senior Night, at my final home game for Nimitz. He had threatened to not show up, and he said he wouldn't drive my mom, either. (She doesn't feel comfortable driving.) Having her there was important to me, and he knew it. I think DeCarlo must have talked to him, because both my parents showed up that night. Before the game, the school had a little celebration honoring the seniors, and my mom and dad came onto the court for it. I had to give them balloons and flowers, but I ignored my dad and handed the stuff to my mom. It was so awkward, standing there with them, pasting a

71

smile on my face for pictures. My dad looked like he wanted to be anywhere else in the world but inside that gym.

And now here I was, standing in the hall at school, facing the anxiety of having to see him again. When I refused to go meet him, he must have called DeCarlo on his way home, because my brother showed up at school later. "Baby girl, just come with me," he said. "Just come talk to him for a little bit. And then I'll bring you back to school." I didn't want to go, but I would do anything for my brother, so I got in the car with him and he drove me to the house. As soon as we pulled into the driveway, I put my head into my hands and burst into tears. I was crushed, just crushed. I used to be daddy's little girl, and now I felt like someone he didn't love or want anymore. Being around him, feeling his disappointment, was a constant reminder of what we had lost.

It was so hard walking into that house. But I did it. I went inside and talked to him. He was sitting in the living room, and I sat with him, and he began saying all these sweet things, about how he was going to let me be who I wanted to be. At first I shook my head, told him I didn't believe him. But I felt worn down, and I missed my mom so much. And the more he kept talking—saying he was sorry, that he just wanted what was best for me, that he was frustrated we never talked anymore, that he wanted things to be right with us again—the more I wanted to believe things could be better with me and him. So I told him I would think about coming home.

I MOVED BACK into the house the following week. My dad gave me my old phone, as well as the keys to the car. It seemed like he was going to be true to his word and support me, all of me. But soon enough, just a couple of weeks later, he started making smart-ass remarks again, saying things like "I hope Baylor still wants you," and "Where you going now, to meet your gay friends?"

I didn't have the stomach to move out again, and I was only a couple of months from graduation. So I stayed. But there was a broken trust between us, and to this day we still bump heads. Whenever it happens, I let him back into my heart, even though I tell myself I won't—even though it has backfired on me a bunch of times.

I'm just not sure I can help it. I guess I'll always be daddy's little girl, wishing things could be the way they used to be.

RUNNING FREE

The drive from Houston to Waco is about three hours, depending on who is driving. I've made it in two and a half, but I have a bit of a heavy foot, as you might imagine (size 17 men's shoe). The day my parents took me to Baylor for the beginning of my freshman season, we drove two cars. My dad led the way, driving his Hummer, and my mom and I followed behind in my Dodge Magnum, which was technically also his car, because he paid for it. I felt like I couldn't get to campus fast enough; the miles ticked by so slowly. I just couldn't wait to start this next part of my life, my big independence. I imagine that's how most college freshmen feel, like they're embarking on a great adventure, the whole world suddenly seeming within their reach. Mostly, though, I just wanted to be able to walk through the door every day without an inquisition about where I was going or where I had been, who I was hanging out with, when I would be back.

When we finally got to campus, we carried all my stuff into my dorm room. I was in a suite with the four other freshmen on the team; we each had our own room and shared a common space. Picture me standing there, bouncing from one foot to the next, antsy, like I had to pee—except what I really wanted was for my parents to leave. I was thinking to myself, *Y'all can go now. Bye, bye. See ya!* But I didn't say that, obviously, because my mom was clearly struggling, not wanting to say good-bye to her baby. She immediately began unpacking my bags. She pulled out my sheets to make the bed. I was going to tell her not to worry about it, but she likes doing that stuff for me. If I had asked her to leave everything, she would have worried that my room would stay in disarray, bags sloppy and unpacked, nothing where I needed it. And she probably would have been right. Plus, I knew she wanted to delay the inevitable, stretch out our time together. So I let her set up my whole dorm room, even down to tucking my socks away in the drawer. I did not touch a bag or a piece of clothing. I just stood to the side with my dad, talking about superficial things like football and the weather. Once the last suitcase was stored in the closet and everything was squared away, Mom realized there was nothing left for her to do; nothing else needed her touch. I remember watching her and thinking she looked like she didn't know what to do with her hands. Finally she laced them together and looked at us with a shrug, as if to say, *Everything is finished.*

"I'll walk you out," I said to my parents. I think maybe they wanted me to invite them for lunch, but I would have spent the whole time checking my watch, wanting to be free of them, and they would have been eating slowly, hoping I'd invite them to stay for dinner, too. It was better to say good-bye quickly and cleanly, like pulling off a Band-Aid. We walked to the Hummer so I could send them off and get on with my day. But then, out of nowhere, a wave of emotion came over me. I felt like I had a basketball lodged in my throat. I looked at my dad, who had his hand on his brow, covering his eyes. He was doing the thing he does when he's trying not to cry, puffing himself out, as if steeling himself. A tear came down his cheek, and seeing him so sad shocked me. I looked at my mom, who was a total goner, just dripping tears like a leaky faucet, her eyes bloodshot. She was a mess.

I really couldn't say much, because I just wanted the moment to pass. I hugged them both, hard, and watched them climb into the Hummer. They were waving and blowing kisses. My chest was heaving, like I couldn't breathe right, and I started crying, too. Standing there, in those few seconds, I felt pure loneliness—the kind you sometimes feel when you're in transition and everything seems to be changing. I was watching my childhood drive away, and I wasn't sure what college life had in store for me. Before the Hummer was out of sight, I turned and ran toward the dorm, stopping just around the corner from the parking lot. I rubbed the back of my hand across my eyes and wiped away the tears. I took a few deep breaths, calming myself, then walked into the dorm to meet my new roommates.

"All right!" I said. "What are we doing now? Let's go to the mall or something. Any parties tonight?"

PRESEASON TRAINING FOR BASKETBALL wasn't that bad. But then again, I'm not one of those people who can't sleep at night because they're worrying about an important meeting or a big test—or, in my case, a killer early morning workout. I usually sleep like a baby, no matter what the next day holds. So even though I remember workouts being difficult while I was actually doing them, I didn't walk around campus thinking about how hard everything was physically. When it comes to the pain of training, I have no short-term memory. I show up the next day and say, "What are we doing this time?"

But one workout does stand out in my mind: the timed mile from my freshman season. Before the first day of actual on-court basketball practice, everyone on the team has to run a mile in a certain amount of time, depending on what position you play. I'm not into distance running. I don't really understand the concept of taking off from one spot, running for a while, then ending up exactly where you started. I'll run all day on the court, because it serves a purpose. But running a mile for the sake of running a mile? That qualifies as "long distance" in my book—especially if you run it in skateboarding sneakers, which is exactly what happened to me.

In the days leading up to our final conditioning test, the coaches had reminded us to take our running sneakers from the locker room, because the gym would be closed on the morning of the timed mile. They had said it repeatedly: "Get your sneakers for the run. Don't forget your sneakers. Everybody get your sneakers." So of course I forgot my sneakers. They were locked away, along with my basketball sneakers, and I didn't realize it until the morning of the run. I woke up around seven that day, because we had to be at the track by eight. And as I was getting dressed, I suddenly had a sinking feeling. I looked around the floor of my dorm room: there were clothes and books, a gym bag, but no running sneakers. All I had were a pair of flip-flops and my black Vans. *Shit!* I didn't think Coach Mulkey would be too happy if I said I couldn't run the mile because I didn't have the right sneakers. That's like saying, "The dog ate my homework." So I made a quick decision: *Screw it, I'll run in my Vans.* I grabbed them, sat on my bed, and laced them up as tightly as I could.

All five of us—me and the other freshmen—piled into my

Dodge Magnum. As we walked to the car, one of my teammates said, "Um, Brittney, where are your shoes?"

"I left them in the gym," I said, unlocking my car and settling into the driver's seat. "I know you all said to get them, but I forgot. So I'm wearing these."

My teammates laughed and rolled their eyes. They were already learning how I can be a little forgetful at times. But hey, at least I can improvise.

It was still kind of dark—the sun was just starting to rise—as we rolled toward the Baylor track, which is located off campus. (The school is now building a new track on campus.) We parked and walked toward the infield, where the coaches were waiting, wearing their Baylor polo shirts and sweats. I think we were all feeling a little uneasy, because this was the first chance for us to really prove ourselves to them, to show we were ready for college ball. Also, it's not like any of us were excited to run the mile. It's just one of those things you have to do before you can get to the good stuff and start hooping.

As the five of us made our way to the starting line, some of the juniors and seniors on the team spotted my Vans and began laughing, giving me a hard time, saying things like "Freshman trying to run in those!" I played along, but the jokes just motivated me even more. I told myself if there are people in Africa who can run marathons barefoot, I can run a mile in a pair of Vans. Coach Mulkey had brought three guys to the track who would serve as our pacesetters, our rabbits, with each of them running a specific time, as fast as we all needed to go. The goal was 6:45 to 7:00 minutes for the guards, 7:30 for the forwards, and 8:00 for the post players like me. Kim explained that if we stayed near the guy pacing our group, we would make our time.

Each coach was holding a stopwatch, adding even more pres-

79

sure to the whole thing. When it was time to run, I lined up on the inside lane, right in the front. I didn't care that I was supposed to be slower than the guards. I had decided I was going to sprint that damn mile, and I didn't care if I needed to be carried off the track afterward. There were more than fifteen of us, along with the guys, packed on the starting line. And when Kim gave us the signal—"Go!"—and all the coaches started their watches, I took off around the first corner like I was being chased by angry dogs.

We had done some longer sprint workouts in advance of the mile. Our strength coach took us through 100-yard and 200-yard repeats, just so we were prepared to run a little longer, because most of the other stuff we did was on the basketball court: quick and short, stop and start. After each lap that morning, each quarter mile, the coaches would call out how much time had passed, and whether we were on pace or needed to pick it up. I tried to ignore everything, including the time, and just ran as hard as I could. I kept a strong, steady pace through the first three laps, and once I hit the line again to start the fourth and final lap, I gave it everything I had.

I crossed the finish line in about seven minutes flat, beating most of the forwards and even a few of the guards. I stopped running immediately, walked a few steps out of the way, and just fell down on the ground, lying on my back and staring at the sky. My lungs felt like they might explode, and my feet were barking at me. A trainer came over and said, "Good job, but get up! Don't cramp up!" I wanted to yell, "I don't care—let me cramp!" But I pulled myself up and staggered over to where the coaches were standing. I heard one of the trainers whisper to another, "She just ran that time, and in Vans?"

I had also eaten Skittles for breakfast.

MY FRESHMAN YEAR AT BAYLOR, I was always doing something. It was like I was trying to pack an entire life, everything I had missed out on, into every weekend. I often felt confined, almost trapped, in high school because my dad needed to know where I was at all times, and because he knew so many people, being a cop. When I thought about college, it was like picturing myself on a narrow road that suddenly opened up into a five-lane highway, and I could punch the gas and really start living life. That day when my parents dropped me off, after we said our good-byes, I wasn't just trying to push away my sadness when I walked back to the dorm and started asking about parties. I was ready to let loose. And that's exactly what I did, full throttle. I was burning the candle at both ends, something that would eventually catch up with me toward the end of my sophomore year.

Of course, basketball came first. Everything I did revolved around my obligations to the team, our practice schedule, our games. At the time, though, I wasn't taking into account how important it was to rest and recharge whenever I could. I was nineteen years old, and in a new place where I could flop into bed after a long night, pull myself up a few hours later, go to classes, and still have a strong practice. I had been raised by a man who wouldn't let me ride my bike anywhere except in circles around our cul-de-sac, so I couldn't resist the urge—it felt like a necessity, really—to put down the windows of my Dodge Magnum and cruise the highway to somewhere else, anywhere else, usually with one or two friends with me. That's how I ended up spending a lot of my free weekends as a freshman. When we didn't have a game or practice, you could often find me in Austin (I spent a lot of time on Sixth Street) or Dallas, partying at the clubs. It didn't matter that both cities are about a two-hundred-mile round trip from Waco. Even during the week, I would go out around campus.

81

Looking back now, I realize I was rebelling against my dad, doing everything opposite of how he would want. Whenever he visited me in Waco, one of the first things he would do is check the miles on the Dodge. He would lean into the front seat and write down the odometer number on some small piece of paper he carried around in his wallet, then compare the new number with the one above it, from his previous visit. Sometimes between visits, he would call me and ask, "How many miles are on the car?" And I would have to walk out to the parking garage and check the odometer. If the number was higher than he expected, he would say, "You drove five hundred miles in a few days?" I would try to give him a lower number, just to avoid the conversation, but it was hard to know how many miles had been on the car the last time he checked. And I wasn't about to start keeping track of it myself. That would just make me paranoid like him.

One time on my way into Austin, I accidentally went through a toll without paying, and my dad received a notice in the mail. He called me and asked where I had been that weekend. I told him I hung out with my teammate Shanay. She was from the Austin area, but I clearly made it sound like we had spent the weekend in Waco. He pounced on me right away. "I know you're lying," he said. "You were in Austin. I got a notice about the toll." I tried to talk my way out of it by saying I meant all along that we were in Austin, and that he just hadn't heard me right. But he was annoyed I lied, and I was annoyed he was still trying to monitor my whereabouts, using the only weapon at his disposal: the odometer on the Dodge Magnum.

Another time I went down to Galveston with some friends, for the gay pride parade, because I had never been to a pride event before. I went home to Houston, parked the Dodge at the house of a good friend from high school, then rode with some other folks. My dad called while we were walking along the beach. He knew I had come to Houston—I wasn't sneaking around—so when he called and asked what I was doing, I told him the truth, that I had gone down to Galveston for the pride festivities. Well, apparently that was the wrong answer, too, because he started in on me again. He said, "Where the hell is my car?" And when I told him where I had left it, he just got madder. "What if I needed to service it?" He was always making excuses about the car. But none of it was really about the car. In this case, he didn't like my friend. He thought she was turning me out—you know, making me gay.

A lot of times with my dad, he doesn't actually say what he means, what he really wants. He uses other people, or things like his car, as his way of trying to get what he wants. So, for example, if I didn't go home to visit for a few weekends, he would call and say, "You're disappointing your mother. She misses you." But then I would call my mom, and she'd say, "Baby Girl, you live your life! I'm doing just fine!" My dad could never just say to me, "Brittney, I love you and miss you. I would love to see you." If he had actually said that to me, I would have gotten in the car and driven home. Instead, everything was always about something else—something I wasn't doing the way he thought I should be doing it. And it was exhausting, always trying to read between the lines, feeling like I needed to keep my guard up at all times.

That Dodge Magnum was his tool, like a GPS locator, and he used it to keep tabs on me, to continue wielding power over my life.

THE PUNCH

I've watched "the punch" at least a dozen times on YouTube. I grimace every time I see it, squinting my eyes as if somehow trying to change the outcome. Most people are spared the misfortune of having their most embarrassing moment captured on video: mine was broadcast live on television, then replayed on the news, then uploaded to the Internet for everyone to see, a cautionary tale for the masses. And yet even if I could press a button and make that clip disappear forever, I wouldn't do it. Because as bad as that moment looks on-screen—and it was a whole lot worse in person—I know now that it was one of the best things to ever happen to me.

When I was younger, the anger and frustration inside me often felt like a living, breathing thing, like a fish caught on a hook, thrashing about, demanding to be released. And a lot of times, the way I chose to release it only made things worse. Instead of the fish swimming away, it stayed in the boat, flopping around and making a mess. I used to believe fighting was a way for me to control things that felt out of my control. I was trying to take back the power, to show everyone they couldn't just say whatever they wanted about me and trample on my feelings. But I've learned over the years that there are painful consequences for letting my emotions fester, and the real turning point came on March 3, 2010, when I punched Jordan Barncastle during a game at Texas Tech. In the days and weeks that followed, I would come to realize I wasn't in control at all, and that allowing my anger to own me was actually making me more vulnerable, not less.

WHAT MOST PEOPLE don't realize is that the confrontation with Jordan Barncastle actually started a couple of weeks earlier during a game in Waco. Texas Tech was playing a smaller lineup, and Barncastle was guarding me for long stretches of the game, which was a mismatch because she's six inches shorter than I am. To make up for the size difference, she started catching me with elbows, hitting me when the referees weren't looking, just doing some of the dirty stuff that happens on the basketball court. I like to talk trash when I play, get inside an opponent's head, so she's thinking about what I'm saying instead of what she should be doing. But I'm not a dirty player. There's no point to it, not with my size. Why give away the advantage I have by getting caught throwing elbows or grabbing someone's shirt? It's not like I can easily hide out there. At the same time, though, I have to protect myself. I can't just let people hang on me and push me around, especially if the refs are swallowing their whistles. If someone gets physical with me, I will get more physical, too.

Barncastle didn't like it when I started pushing back. I don't know if maybe she thought she could get away with it because I'm taller, as if these little tricks were her way of evening things out, to make it more fair. Coach Mulkey used to get so upset with the refs, because this kind of thing happened more and more as my career went along. It was like the refs had a different set of criteria for fouls when I was on the court. I would have players all over me, double-teams, triple-teams, and they practically had to drag me to the ground before we could get the call. I think that's just a fact of life for big, dominant post players. Look at Shaquille O'Neal: he got mauled out there. It's almost as if the refs have this mind-set, whether it's conscious or not, that a normal foul—a slap or a shove—isn't a foul when someone is guarding a much bigger player. So, anyway, Barncastle and I went at each other hard that first game, and at one point she walked away from me to complain to the ref that things were getting too physical. When she walked back, I said to her, "You think the referee is going to save you?" And then when I scored on her, drawing a foul, too, I called out, "And one!" (We would eventually get a warning from the ref, telling us both to take it down a notch.) I don't buy the idea that female athletes need to be nice and ladylike on the court. The heat of competition burns just as hot for a woman as it does for a man.

When we played Texas Tech in Lubbock two weeks later, a couple of our assistant coaches pulled me aside beforehand and said, "Don't get into it with Barncastle this time." I told them I wouldn't. But once the game started, it was the same aggressive stuff, pushing and pulling, locking arms, elbows to the body. We were both just going at it again, except now instead of talking trash back at me, she was walking over to the refs during most dead balls, complaining about me. That probably got under my skin a lot more than if we had just kept getting tangled. If you want to dish it out, the way she was dishing it out, you should be able to take it when somebody gives it back. She was playing really aggressive defense, so I was doing the same thing.

And then it got ugly. I made it ugly. We were winning by 16 points, with about nine minutes left in the game, and I was posting up on the low block, using my arms and elbows to get position on her and call for the ball. I remember hearing the referee's whistle and keeping my arms up, because she was still hanging all over me. She grabbed my arm and kind of whipped me around, throwing me out of the play. The foul was clearly on her; the play should have been over. But it wasn't over for me, not inside my head. I was kind of twisted down, still on my feet but wrapped around myself, eyes facing the red-painted wood of the court—and all of a sudden I snapped. A second earlier, I could hear the buzz of the fans, the squeaking of sneakers, the sharp whistle of the referee. But as I rose up tall again, on the spot where she had flung me, everything was a blur. The crowd fell out of view, the other players disappeared from the court, and I couldn't hear or see anybody else except for Jordan Barncastle, in her white-and-red uniform. It was just the two of us. We'd been dancing that line all game, like a pair of boxers, but I had managed to channel my energy and frustration into making big plays. Now all I cared about was hitting her, making her fall. That was the thought flashing through my mind in one split second: *Make her fall.* I whipped my right arm around and tried to connect. It could have been a lot worse. I mean, it was bad enough—I would find out later that I broke her nose—but, thankfully, I didn't hit her square and catch her with my knuckles. I could have done serious damage.

The second after I hit her, as my arm was still following through, I snapped back to reality, and I knew right away that everything was about to change. I heard the crowd. I heard the boos. I heard the thoughts racing through my head. *Shit. I just really fucked up. This is bad. This is bad. Damn. Damn. Damn. This is my biggest fuckup ever*. I don't even think I could wrap my mind around how big of a mistake it was, how it would haunt me in the years to come. I didn't have any of that perspective yet—I could still feel the anger bubbling inside me—but I knew instantly that it was serious, that I had messed up in a huge way.

Coach Damion came onto the court and wrapped me up. "All right, B, it's good, it's good," he kept saying. Some of my teammates were going back and forth with players on Texas Tech, so he was worried I might keep fighting. I was ejected from the game, which meant I needed to leave the court. I had punched Barncastle in front of our team's bench, but the tunnel leading to our locker room was at the other end of the court, so I had to walk in front of their bench, then underneath the fans who were sitting in the corner seats by the tunnel. Damion walked on one side of me, and our strength and conditioning coach was on the other side. I still hadn't spoken to Kim yet; I hadn't even looked over at her after the play, because I was scared to see her reaction.

"Damn, you got her," Damion said to me while we were walking.

"I know."

"Damn," he repeated, shaking his head. "We're going to get through this, though."

"I hope so," I said, keeping my head down as we walked through the entrance of the tunnel, because I was really worried someone would throw something at us. I'm not sure how I would have reacted to that, but I was feeling cornered and on edge, jumpy almost, so I knew I didn't want to find out.

Damion was trying to reassure me that we would handle whatever fallout came from my actions. I didn't think Kim would kick me off the team, but I was worried the NCAA might suspend me for enough games that my season would be finished. We had only one regular-season game left, so even a five-game suspension would mean I'd miss the entire Big 12 tournament and maybe the first two rounds of the NCAA tourney, making it a lot tougher for my team to advance. There wasn't much precedent for how the NCAA would handle the situation, and I was worried they'd come down hard on me to make a statement.

There were several minutes left in the game, so Damion couldn't stay with me in the locker room. He told me to hang tight as he turned and walked back to the court. I untucked my jersey, letting it hang over my shorts. I rummaged through my bag for my cell phone, then sank into the chair I had sat in before the game. I didn't dare take off my uniform. I knew if Kim came back into the locker room and saw me in my sweats, looking like I had separated myself from the team instead of sticking it out until the very end, she would be angry and disappointed in a whole new way. I leaned forward and untied my sneakers, but I didn't take them off. When I pulled up the score of the game on my phone, I saw Texas Tech was making a run, coming from behind, and I could hear the muffled excitement from the crowd. Everybody was texting me, too. Someone sent me a message telling me the clip had already been uploaded to YouTube. I dropped my head and stared at the space between my sneakers. *How did I get myself here?* There was also a text from my dad saying I should have kept fighting. He was angry that after all the back and forth between me and Barncastle, I was the one who got tossed. Of course I was also the one who punched her in the nose.

After a few minutes, our team manager, Jordin Westbrook, came into the locker room. I looked at her and asked, "They making a run?"

"Yeah, they scored a couple of times," she said.

"Did it look that bad?" I knew she would know exactly what I meant.

"Uh . . . yes," she answered. "It looked horrible."

"Did I actually get her?"

I could not sit still as a kid. I don't know who I'm calling in this picture, but it was probably someone with a car.

This is me at age five. Sweet as can be, right? (Sometimes!)

I was usually on my best behavior when my mom and I stopped by my grandparents' house in Houston. But don't be fooled: I was a handful as a ten-year-old.

One of the few things I liked about moving to the country (temporarily) during middle school: being a badass on my four-wheeler.

That's my "big" sister Pier with me and my parents when I was in high school. We fought a lot as kids, but she watched out for me as I got older.

Even though I had grown to six foot eight by the time I was seventeen, a part of me was still Daddy's little girl.

I was so happy to be done with high school. I would have been even happier if I didn't have to wear a dress underneath my graduation gown.

My Dodge Magnum gave me freedom—until my dad started keeping track of every mile I put on it in college.

I loved coming home to Houston and hanging out with my nephew, EJ, especially when my mom was in the kitchen making ice cream for us.

It wasn't so easy to be myself at Baylor, but I could always count on my "sis" Janell to put a smile on my face when she came to visit.

I broke my wrist skateboarding during my junior year at Baylor. But hey, at least it happened after we won the national championship. Phew.

My Baylor bros Nash (*left*) and Julio (*right*) joined me at the 2012 ESPY Awards. Frosting on the cake: I took home the trophy for Female Athlete of the Year.

Stepping forward as the No. 1 pick in the 2013 WNBA Draft felt amazing, thanks to an assist from a stylist. (You can't see here, but I'm wearing white Chuck Taylor sneakers, too.)

Training camp with the Phoenix Mercury took a cool turn when Kareem Abdul-Jabbar showed up to give me some pointers on how to shoot his legendary skyhook. (And yes, I need more practice.)

I dunked twice in my first WNBA game. Unfortunately, I also got into foul trouble and we lost to the Chicago Sky, setting the tone for my up-and-down rookie season.

My life was a whirlwind after I turned pro. One of the highlights: a trip to Nike's indoor skate park in LA, where I met (*from left to right*) C. R. Stecyk III, Eric Koston, and Lance Mountain, three legends of the skateboarding scene.

Keeping my speed in check wasn't a problem during my stop at Nike. I've learned my lesson!

Now that we're teammates, I see every day why Diana Taurasi is one of the all-time best players in our sport—because her basketball IQ is through the roof. She's like a coach out on the court.

Power tie meets power tiger: NBA commissioner David Stern and I compare outfits at the annual WNBA Inspiring Women Luncheon. He's retired now, but he's still a huge supporter of our league.

I wasn't sure yet if I had really hurt Barncastle, because I knew I didn't make direct contact. Jordin told me there was cotton stuffed up Barncastle's nose and that it didn't look right. We sat in silence for a few more minutes, waiting for the game to end. By that time, our team had hit a couple of big buckets, and we were clearly going to win. But those were long minutes for me. I was dreading the storm that was coming my way, once the final buzzer sounded. I could feel it, hear it, heading directly for me, as my teammates jogged down the hallway, the sound of their sneakers getting louder and louder. I looked at Jordin and made my eyes big, like, *This is it.*

The locker room door swung open and everyone filled in around me, sweaty and out of breath. I could hear the clicking of Kim's heels in the hallway. She walked through the doorway and stood at the front of the room. I was sitting as still as possible, holding my breath, like I was trying to make myself disappear.

"That is totally unacceptable!"

I could feel Kim's eyes on me, like lasers, as she yelled. "I'll deal with your ass when we get back to Waco!"

Everyone was quiet as we showered and got ready to leave the arena. My teammates didn't really say too much about what had happened, probably because they didn't want to be seen talking with me right at the moment—guilt by association and all. A few of them said, under their breath, "Damn, B, right in the nose." And later, months afterward, they would turn "Barncastle" into a verb. If we were going hard during a scrimmage, someone would say, "Don't Barncastle me." I think we all knew that the best way to deal with it, to put it behind me, was to acknowledge it, instead of pretending it never happened.

I HAD A MEETING IN Kim's office the day after we got back from Lubbock. The NCAA had handed down a one-game suspension, and Kim decided to add on another game, to show everyone how seriously she was taking the incident. She also tacked on a number of obligations—most of which were not made public—as part of my punishment. I had to write a letter of apology to Jordan Barncastle. I had to put in a certain number of hours doing community service, which meant I spent many afternoons and weekends working at a soup kitchen, serving food to the homeless. And I had to see a therapist, a requirement I initially rolled my eyes at, assuming it would be the kind of thing you see on television: *And how did that make you feel?*

I sat in Kim's office, and we talked about what had happened. She explained she had to take a tough stance, to make it clear she wouldn't tolerate that kind of behavior, because what I had done was wrong, and now I had to go about making it right. But she also said she understood how frustrating it was to be me on the court. She saw how much abuse I absorbed without getting the same calls as players smaller than I am. "You just can't retaliate," she stressed. "The blame always falls on the player who retaliates."

I knew she was right. But here's the thing: you don't always understand something right away just because someone explains it. Kim and the other coaches had said all along that I needed to keep my cool, that I would have to deal with a lot of crap on the court, players trying to knock me down to their size. I would nod my head—yup, yup, yup—then step onto the court and push all that advice out of my mind. It wasn't until I punched Jordan Barncastle that the message really hit home for me. That game at Texas Tech would be the last one I played without constantly reminding myself I needed to stay level-headed.

We ended up reaching the Final Four that spring (we lost in the semifinals to Connecticut, the eventual national champion), and I finished the season averaging 18.4 points and 8.5 rebounds per game. I wanted so much to redeem myself, to put the punch behind me, while also trying to learn from it. The hardest part was that nobody really understood my history of fighting. I think Kim knew, just from us talking here and there, that I had some conflicts when I was younger—"altercations," she called them. But nobody at Baylor, and certainly nobody in the media, had any idea how much I had struggled as a kid, trying to solve my problems and hide my insecurities by fighting. That was my response to feeling vulnerable when I was young: raising my fists.

TOWARD THE END OF middle school, and even into my freshman year of high school, before I fully dedicated myself to basketball, I wanted to be a real fighter, the kind who steps into a ring or a cage. I didn't know how good I would become at hoops, but I knew I needed an outlet for my emotions, a way to release all my pent-up energy. So I talked to my dad about getting a punching bag and some gear, because I wanted to try boxing. I also raised the idea of MMA and ultimate fighting, but my mom absolutely refused to allow it. (See? She did put her foot down on occasion—and I can't blame her for that.) She could barely understand why I wanted to box.

My dad put the speed bag, punching bag, dumbbells, and hand wraps in a section of our family room, and I would come home from school and work out. I'm an adrenaline junkie, a thrill seeker, so I really connected with the emotional intensity of boxing. Sometimes Dad would come in and hold the punching bag for me. It even got to the point where we talked about getting me some lessons. But Mom was scared; she didn't want me to get hurt. She begged me, and my dad, not to pursue it beyond the family room. So my boxing career was short-lived, although I continued to hit the bag and use the weights throughout high school.

The punching bag was made of this rough material, and I had to wrap my knuckles before practicing. But one time I came home

93

after school and went crazy on the bag, without wrapping my hands. I was steamed about something (I can't remember what), and the next thing I knew, the punching bag was red and my mom was shrieking, "Oh my God, my baby's hands!" I was like, "Mom, chill, it's okay." Another time I punched the bag so hard, the stand it was on swung backward and put a hole in the wall. I didn't know I was that strong.

IN THE YEARS after "the punch," the story line became that I had made this one mistake and it was totally out of character for me. *She's just a big teddy bear. A gentle giant.* I was glad people were willing to forgive what I had done (well, except for the online trolls who still bring it up), but I also felt a little uncomfortable with how simplified everything was—all neat and tidy and fixed—when the reality was that I had worked hard to control my anger.

Kim wanted me to see the therapist every week for the rest of the school year. As I drove to his office for that first visit, I told myself that it was just another obligation, something I had to do to check the box and move on. I wasn't planning to say much, because I'm stubborn like that: I thought therapists were for people who are weak, and I didn't need to see a shrink. I was still learning that the weakest people are the ones who can't ask for help. His office was off campus, unaffiliated with Baylor. There were two large windows in the corner, facing leafy green trees and shrubs. I sat in a leather chair with little pleats in it. (I spent a lot of time fiddling with those stitches.) The therapist sat on the couch, and the first thing he said to me was, "So how are you doing? How was your day?" I had been expecting him to ask me why I punched Jordan Barncastle and if I felt bad about it. I thought the whole thing would be weird and awkward. I remember feeling stiff, ready to shut down. And then he asked me that simple question, as if he really cared about how I was doing, and I felt myself relax into that leather chair. I also liked that he said, "If you want to cuss, go ahead and cuss. It doesn't matter what you want to say, just say it. I'm here to listen. I want to listen. So tell me what you want to talk about."

We just had a conversation. And it didn't take him long, maybe it was the second or third session, to figure out that so much of who I am, of how I act and how I respond and how much anger I feel sometimes, is a direct result of my relationship with my dad. That first session, the therapist asked me about my family, and he noticed how I kind of changed—my body language, the emotion in my voice—when I started talking about my father. So we stayed on that topic longer, and when we circled back around to it, the same thing happened.

Starting therapy is like pointing a spotlight into your past and into your heart. Although I initially went because of what happened at Texas Tech, it became an important part of my life away from basketball. I stayed in Waco for school that summer, and I stayed in therapy, too. I kept going back throughout my sophomore year, then on and off for the rest of college. At first Kim would check in with me to make sure I was going on a regular basis, but she quickly backed off once she realized I was taking it seriously. As time passed, I would go depending on how I felt each week. If I was stressed about something, I would schedule a session. If things were going smoothly, I'd still try to make time for it every couple of weeks.

It didn't bother me if people knew I was seeing a therapist. A few of my teammates had to see him, too, and they hated it. I would try to tell them, "Just talk to the man! He's not trying to make you do anything. He just wants to hear how things are going." My therapist provided me with a certain peace of mind. When I became angry about something that happened with basketball, or school, or my dad, I would go talk to him and calm down. Whatever the situation, he helped me look at it in a better way, and he encouraged me to move past the anger I held on to. That has always been my Achilles' heel: letting wrongs and slights fester inside me instead of discussing them right away. I'll tell everyone that everything is fine, until things are so far past fine that I'm about to burst with anger or sadness.

Finding a great therapist was the silver lining that came from the Jordan Barncastle incident. I don't know how I would have made it through my sophomore year, and the swirl of depression I found myself in, without having that support.

96

TO THE MOON AND BACK

The summer after my freshman year, I was hanging out in my dorm room one afternoon when I saw that my mom was calling my cell phone. It wasn't unusual for her to call—we talked a few times a week—because she liked to check in and see how things were going. But the moment I picked up the phone and said, "Hey, Mom," I could tell by the energy on the other end that something wasn't right. I immediately stood up, because I wanted to feel taller and more in control. I could hear she was crying. And then I found out why: she told me she had gone to the doctor and they had found something. She'd been diagnosed with lupus, which I later learned is an auto-immune disease. My mom's immune system was "hyperactive" and attacking her healthy cells. The diagnosis explained a lot, because her health was always an issue, but hearing she had a disease was really scary. It made her struggles seem so much more real, to know exactly what was going on inside her body and what she would have to deal with going forward.

I walked out of my dorm room. I needed to keep moving; it helped me process what she was saying. I was trying to be really strong for her, and I told her, my voice steady, "Okay, Mom, you'll be okay. Do you hear me? Everything is going to be okay. You can fight this." I walked into the parking garage, pacing around the same area where I had said a teary good-bye to my parents the previous fall, and then I headed over to the little grassy area outside the dorm. I listened as she cried and talked about her worries, and I kept trying to reassure her that everything would be okay.

As soon as we said good-bye, as soon as we hung up, I broke down. There was a seating area under the trees outside the dorm, and I made my way over to one of the chairs and lowered myself into it. I buried my face in my hands and just sobbed, feeling totally helpless. But there was something else, too, another emotion mixed in with my fear and sadness: it was guilt. I started thinking about all the trouble I had given my mother when I was a kid, constantly mouthing off and disobeying her, just to see how far I could push her. I had never made things easy on her. And now I wanted nothing more than to ease her pain, to provide comfort and support. Why had I taken her for granted?

I looked down at my phone. I needed to tell someone, talk it through, and I didn't even hesitate when I hit the number. The line rang a couple of times, and then I heard Kim's voice in my ear. "Hey, Big Girl," she said with her southern twang. I broke down again, crying, telling Kim everything my mom had told me. She listened and tried to provide some support, playing the role for me that I had just played for my mom. She told me to come over to her house if I needed a place to chill. "Everything is going to be fine," Kim said. "You need to be strong for your mom."

We stayed on the phone for a couple of minutes as I pulled myself together. "All right," I told Kim. "I will. I can do that."

A few days later, I went to see my therapist, and talking through it with him helped me a lot. I told him I was worried about my mom and also distracted by the guilt I felt for the way I had treated her when I was younger. He encouraged me to put it all out there: if something was weighing on my heart, I should talk to her about it. I had been checking in with her every day or two, just to say hi and see how she was feeling. But after seeing my therapist, I knew I needed to say more.

ONE AFTERNOON, about a week after my mom had called to tell me about the lupus, I was lying on my bed, staring at the ceiling, working up the nerve to call her, thinking about all the things I wanted to say to her. I knew it would be an emotional conversation, but I also knew it was something I needed to do. My mom was always battling some kind of physical ailment when I was a kid. She had a couple of back surgeries for a bulging disk, which left her with nerve damage, and she had a lot of problems with her left knee. She was in constant pain, which made it hard for her to get out much. On top of everything else, she also just seemed to have bad luck. I remember when I was little, she had a mishap while lighting the grill, and she ended up in the hospital with burns on her face. She is the sweetest person in the world, but it's like she has a black cloud following her around. And dealing with me all those years probably zapped a lot of her energy.

We talked for about ninety minutes that day, and I apologized for every stupid thing I had done as a kid, for being such a troublemaker, for being just plain mean to her. It was an epic heart-to-heart conversation. I was crying; she was crying. She likes to call me "Baby

Girl" and "Ladybug," and when she started dropping those on me, I was just a puddle. I was sitting there going through my laundry list of bad behavior, and she was saying things like "Everything is good, Baby Girl," her voice all soft and warm. We shared our favorite memories, and I told her how I was learning—in fits and starts—to deal with my emotions better. And when we had both said everything we needed to say, we ended the call with this line we always say to each other: "I love you to the stars and back, to the moon and back."

My mom and I are different in a lot of ways, but ever since that phone call, she has become one of my best friends. Sometimes when we're talking, I'll think back to those times when she was sitting in the recliner chair, watching the Food Network, with me sprawled across her lap—and I'm reminded all over again that I'm still her Ladybug.

KEEP IT BEHIND CLOSED DOORS

My sophomore year at Baylor sucked. There's really no better way to say it. Everything felt like a struggle. The tone was set over the summer, when I found out from my mom that she had lupus, and I just could never quite pull myself out of the quicksand. I clashed with Kim, I clashed with my dad, I clashed with the girl I was dating, I clashed with Baylor.

Most of all, I clashed with myself.

Basketball was the easy part, although I found plenty of ways to make it harder. My teammates and I—specifically, the other sophomores—were a handful. Coming out of high school, we were ranked as the top recruiting class in the country, and when we arrived in Waco, we acted like we were above the law. Kim's law, that is. Freshman year, I was late to everything—classes, tutoring sessions, study hall. And if I wasn't late, I was showing up at the last minute. (When you play college basketball, "on time" usually means fifteen minutes early.) There were a few of us in Kim's doghouse, which meant we spent the summer on permanent workout probation. Every morning, we had to be in the weight room, dressed and ready to go, at 6 A.M., under the supervision of our strength and conditioning coach. Technically, these sessions were considered punishment, an extra hour of sweat in addition to our regular team workout later in the day. But I didn't look at it that way. As much as I hated getting up at the crack of dawn, I also saw these sessions as a chance to get stronger. At least that's what I told myself while we were being tortured.

I'm not one of those people who can always remember specific drills I've been forced to do; usually I just go all out and forget about what happened the moment it ends. But there was one particular lifting drill we did during those early-morning sessions that is burned into my muscle memory. I'm sure once I describe it, people will think it doesn't sound all that hard. Trust me, it was. (Go ahead and try it.) We held a small weight in each hand—like maybe five pounds—and we had to keep our elbows locked as we raised our arms until they met at the top. Picture the arm motion of a jumping jack, except we had to do it slowly and in rhythm with everyone else. The goal was to complete 100 repetitions. But here's the catch: if anyone bent her elbows, even just a smidge, we had to start all over again. And of course that is what happened. We'd get so close, like 95 reps, and somebody would screw up. We did three sets, and I would guess that by the time we finished the last one, we had actually done about 500 arm raises.

THE BASKETBALL COURT has always been the one place I feel free, not weighed down by outside worries. Some people can't turn off their minds when they're playing; they're still stressed about everything happening off the court. I'm not like that. In fact, I couldn't wait to get on the court and play sophomore year, because I was really struggling away from the game. Sometimes I would even go to the gym late at night, when I couldn't sleep, just to shoot and be in that space. (I'd also sit in the locker room and play video games.) There were so many things swirling around me that year, clouding my brain. My dad was still being himself, hovering over me even from Houston. He started harping on one thing in particular: he said I needed a bodyguard. After the final home game of my freshman year, Kim had allowed the fans onto the court, so we could show our appreciation for all their support throughout the season. I was serving my two-game suspension for punching Jordan Barncastle, so I sat in the student section near the Baylor bench. But after the game, I mingled with the crowd on the court. We were swarmed, and I didn't mind it one bit. I had fun signing autographs and posing for pictures; it took some of the sting out of watching my team lose to Texas. But my dad was livid afterward, saying Kim shouldn't have let that happen. "Anyone could have just come up and done you harm," he said. He believed, and still believes to this day, that somebody might run up and stab me on the court. So as I was going into my sophomore season, he would call me and complain about how Baylor did things, telling me I should transfer and that I needed a security detail. (He also thought I wasn't getting enough touches on the court, which is ridiculous. If anything, Kim would get mad at me for passing too much.)

I already had enough internal angst that I processed on a daily basis; I didn't have the capacity to absorb so much of his. Plus, there was my mom's health, which I thought about multiple times a day. I was scared I might lose her. The thought of my mom in pain, sad, struggling, weighed on me, especially since I didn't go

103

home as much as I wanted to, because being in the same house as my dad was too stressful. I would call and check on her all the time. I'd ask how she was feeling, then listen carefully to what she said. She would almost always give the same answer—"Okay"— but I could tell when she was lying because her voice would be softer. When it sounded more like a whisper, I knew she was having a bad day. No matter how much I tried to pry the truth out of her, she would still say everything was fine.

Sometimes I would call my sister Pier and ask her what was really going on, why Mom wouldn't tell me the truth. Pier would say, "She doesn't want you to worry, Baby Girl!" But I did worry. In the absence of real information, I would picture the worst possible scenarios, especially because the information my dad passed along often made it seem as if my mom was dying and I should get in the car immediately and drive home. I remember one time he called and said that Mom had fallen down the stairs in the house and was in bad shape. I hung up and called Pier, and she said Mom had slipped the last step or two and was fine. Sometimes it felt like my father was trying to lay a guilt trip on me, another way he could control my actions and emotions. But I'm sure he had his own fears about losing my mother. We just didn't talk about it.

Meanwhile, I was starting to realize there was another topic that would cause me problems at Baylor: my sexuality. Many people have asked me why I went to Baylor, a private Baptist university, if I knew I was gay. After all, the student handbook has a policy against homosexuality (as well as premarital sex between straight people). The most direct answer I can offer is this: I had zero knowledge of the policy. My parents didn't know about it either. My dad worried in general about me, because he seemed convinced that being openly gay would hurt my basketball career. But nobody on the Baylor coaching staff, and certainly not Kim, alerted me to this important piece of information about the school. Keep in mind, I chose Baylor because of basketball. Also, as I have learned all too well, the world of women's college basketball is a homophobic and hypocritical place: it's not like anyone was going to sit me down and say, "Brittney, we know you're a lesbian, so we want to give you a heads-up about our school's policy on homosexuality." The coaches at Baylor weren't going to do anything to discourage me from coming to play for their program. But equally important, these words—*lesbian, homosexual*—make a lot of people within women's basketball squirm, including all those gay players and coaches in the closet. People want to dance around the subject, pretend it doesn't exist, instead of having open conversations about it.

Here's what I did know: Baylor had an awesome program, it was close to my home, and Kim was a great coach, someone whose personality I thought I could relate to because I had put up with my dad's brand of discipline for so long. There was a lot about Baylor I didn't know, but worrying about the policies and rules of the overall administration felt like worrying about the government in another country. How would that affect me?

Turns out, it would affect me a lot.

THE FIRST TIME I KISSED a girl—like, a real kiss—was my freshman year of high school. In sixth grade, one of my friends and I shared a little peck, just playing around the way kids do, but it's not like either one of us really knew if we were gay. In ninth grade, I knew. There was a girl who lived right around the corner in our neighborhood—she was a few years older than me—and she offered to braid my hair one day. We hit it off and started hanging out sometimes. I remember there being an energy, a connection between us, but I didn't know she felt the same way until this one afternoon, on the way over to her house after school, when we stopped at the store to pick up a few snacks. We were both stand-

105

ing in the aisle, deciding what chips to buy, when she just turned and kissed me on the lips. I didn't know what to say, so I stated the obvious: "You just kissed me." She nodded and smiled. A second later, I leaned in and kissed her again, so she would know for sure that I was not opposed to what was happening. After that, I started spending more time at her house, in her room. I was fifteen by then, but my dad was still paranoid about me going anywhere, so I would sneak over there or tell my mom I was "going to get my hair braided." I'm pretty sure she knew something was up, because I would get my hair done like three times a week.

That was the first time somebody rocked my world. But my friend moved away later that year, and I started dating different girls, nothing serious. I was a bit of a player in high school. I didn't want to get too involved with anyone because I knew it wouldn't last once I got to college. I was a teenager. It's not like I was going to be with someone for years and years and have this fairy-tale ending with the white picket fence.

My first serious relationship began the summer I got to Baylor. This girl had seen me play in the state championship game my senior year, and she messaged me afterward on Facebook. She told me she was going to Baylor that fall, too, and gave me her number so maybe we could meet up and be friends. Normally I wouldn't have responded to something like that, but this time I did, and we started texting, then e-mailing and talking on the phone a lot over the next few months. She sent me some pictures of herself, and I was definitely intrigued. But we never met in person until I got to Waco. We made a plan to spend some time together before classes started. We had agreed to meet face-to-face in the parking lot outside the Ferrell Center, and I was waiting for her, all nervous, leaning against my Dodge Magnum, trying to position myself so I would look as cool as possible. She drove up in her silver Pontiac, and when she stepped out of her car, I saw she was even more beautiful than she looked in the pictures. I think I actually gulped. She had long dark hair, warm brown eyes, and a big smile; she was real natural looking, not a lot of makeup. She gave me a long, lingering hug, and we clicked right away. We spent a lot of time together those next few weeks and months. She would wait for me after games, at the Ferrell Center, and hang out with me at the dorm. My teammates all knew. Lots of people knew, because they'd see us walking together on campus all the time. It was obvious we were a thing.

But like a lot of relationships that burn hot at the beginning, ours ended in flames. Toward the end of freshman year, I found out she was cheating on me, and things got pretty crazy for a while. We broke up, got back together, broke up again, got together again—on and off, on and off—all the way into the fall of sophomore year, until I finally ended it for good. It was just way too much drama, even for me. I was trying to figure out how to reduce the drama in my life, but I was so used to it with my dad, I think I tolerated more of it than some other people might. Also, who doesn't have drama in college? Isn't that part of the learning process, too?

Maybe that's why my next relationship was mostly long distance. I started dating a woman I had met in high school through one of my AAU teammates. She went to college in Atlanta but would come to Baylor every month or two, and we were together until the middle of my senior year. The good part: less drama. The bad part: less quality time. We got to the point where it seemed like we were together almost out of convenience, like neither of us had the desire to improve the relationship or to call it off, either. Eventually we parted ways, just made a clean break (a lot cleaner than my previous breakup), and I decided to chill for a while.

At least, that was the plan. I met my next girlfriend, Cherelle, through a good mutual friend at Baylor. We were all part of the

107

same circle, and Cherelle would invite everybody over to dinner on a regular basis. I really liked talking to her because she was a good listener, thoughtful, smart, somebody who seemed mature and strong. I would tell her about the issues I was having with my girlfriend in Atlanta, how we didn't really seem to connect anymore, and Cherelle could relate because she was on the verge of a breakup herself. She was someone I came to trust more and more over time. And then one day the little lightbulb went off over my head, and I realized I had strong feelings for her. I said to myself, *Ah! I like my friend!* She made me work hard to win her over (we'll get to that later), but we eventually started dating toward the end of my senior year, and her presence in my life was a welcome bright spot when so much was swirling around me.

All of which is to say, I was in relationships for most of my time at Baylor. And I was doing all the typical things that people in relationships do, like going to the movies and out to dinner, sending little shout-outs on social media. It was tame stuff. But I was at a conservative school, and I was one of the more recognizable students on campus, so I ran into some problems. The first "incident" was at the beginning of my sophomore year, during preseason training, before we officially started on-court basketball practice. I sent out a tweet to my girlfriend in Atlanta, something sweet, saying I missed her. That same night, I retweeted a post from an LGBT group that I followed. They had sent out a message—something along the lines of "No More Hate" or "Love One Another for Who You Are"—and I sent it to my followers as well. I didn't give it much thought at the time, because it wasn't anything out of the ordinary on Twitter, but Kim called me into her office the next day. She was sitting behind her desk, and as we were making small talk, I really had no clue why I was there.

"I'm going to need you to take down those messages you posted last night," she said eventually. She described the tweets as "not appropriate" and implied that someone in the compliance office had alerted her. (Every athletic program has a compliance office, to try to make sure coaches and players are following school and NCAA rules.) Kim didn't make it seem like this was up for discussion; I needed to take down the tweets. "We just can't have that stuff out there," I remember her saying. So I shrugged and said fine, okay. And that was basically it.

I went home and immediately deleted the tweets. But the more I thought about it, the angrier I got. *Screw that. Why can't I say what I want?* Then I decided to take things a step further: I changed my screen name, and I blocked everyone in the Baylor program from my account. (I used to keep my Twitter and Instagram accounts private, to avoid the trolls.) Keep in mind, it wasn't like I was sending outrageous messages. I wasn't being stupid or over the top. For someone to actually understand who I was talking to, or what I was talking about, they would have to be paying close attention. It wasn't until my senior year, when I had a public account, that I started dropping more hints, and even then, I was careful about what I wrote.

That meeting in Kim's office was the first time (but not the last time) I got the impression she was worried her program would look bad if people knew she had gay players. And I was confused by that. At the beginning of each season, and then again at various points throughout the year, Kim would give us the same speech: "Keep your business behind closed doors. I don't care what y'all do on your own time, but don't tell the whole world everything about it." I actually agreed with Kim, up to a certain point—until I realized my "business" was viewed differently. After the Twitter incident, I took a look at what some of my straight teammates were saying on their Facebook and Twitter pages, and they were sending messages to their boyfriends or retweeting love quotes or horoscopes or relationship advice. So how come they didn't have to keep their business behind closed doors? Why was I doing something wrong?

DURING MY SOPHOMORE YEAR, I stayed in Waco more often than I did as a freshman. But that doesn't mean I wasn't still running away from something. That year I lived off campus, sharing an apartment with a guy on the track team named Patrick. Being out of the dorm was cool, and I had no shortage of people to hang out with and have a good time. But all too often, there were things happening that dragged me down. Looking back now, I believe I was battling depression that year. The hits just kept on coming, and I was still learning how to handle all my churning emotions. I would see my therapist to talk it out, try to release some of the angst, but there were times it felt like my second skin.

I had gotten my first tattoo during my senior year of high school, just before graduation. My aunt (she wasn't actually my biological aunt, but a friend of the family) took me to the tattoo parlor as a graduation present. When I walked into the shop, I wasn't sure exactly what I wanted, so I flipped through a book to see different examples. I stopped at this image of a crown, except the drawing had a skull and some other decorations at the top. I didn't want anything except the crown. I pointed to that tattoo and said, "Let's do this." Then, a second later: "And let's put a basketball on the top!"

I got it on the back of my left shoulder, and the tattoo artist included my initials. I didn't tell my dad, obviously, because he hates tattoos, but he ended up seeing it on graduation day, as I was walking around the house getting ready. My high school had a rule that all female graduates must wear dresses under their gowns, because apparently the administration didn't get the memo that it's the twenty-first century and some girls would rather go naked than wear a dress. My mom had picked one out for me; it was like a really long tube top, and I felt like I couldn't breathe in it. Anyway, before I had a chance to cover up, my dad happened to catch a glimpse of me in the hall and said, "What the hell is that thing on your shoulder? How long you had that? You gonna mark up your whole damn body?" (Come to think of it, that is another advantage of being tall: more space to get creative with the ink.)

I got my next two tattoos, a matching pair, during my freshman year at Baylor. I was in the weight room one day, and I saw one of the track athletes had stars tattooed onto his calves. They looked cool, and I decided I wanted something like that, so I got them on the front of my shoulders—one red star on either side of my collarbone. My first tattoos were inspired by mostly good emotions; I was just enjoying the moment and feeling compelled by certain images.

That wasn't the case with the tattoo I got my sophomore year at Baylor: two skulls, one laughing, one crying. I wanted something that reflected the conflicting emotions I felt, the pressure of having to act one way in public, then going home and breaking down. (I had intended to go back to the tattoo parlor and get the words "Laugh now, cry later" inscribed next to the skulls, but I never did. It seemed obvious enough already.) I just always felt like certain people wanted to pretend that a big part of me—my sexual identity—didn't exist. Mostly that feeling came from my dad, but a number of incidents happened at Baylor that made me think Kim would prefer not to deal with it either.

The day after Valentine's Day, Kim called me into her office. Things were going well for me with basketball; I had put the Jordan Barncastle incident behind me (even if Big 12 fans reminded me of it every time we played on the road), and I was a team captain. On the court, I felt as strong as I'd ever been. So I figured Kim just wanted to check in with me, like she did sometimes, or talk about the upcoming stretch of games. But instead, she told me she was disappointed in my behavior. I had gone out to dinner with my girlfriend the night before, and somehow it got back to Kim that I was gaying it up in public. That's not the term she used, of course, but apparently someone didn't think it looked good that I was out with another woman, sitting at a table for two, on Valentine's Day. Maybe I touched my girlfriend's hand at one point, or leaned in to tell her something. Maybe we were walking too close together as we were leaving. Who knows? Kim didn't get specific, so I can only imagine what she heard. I'm sure it all sounded like the makings of a soft-core porn film. "Big Girl, you just have to keep your business behind closed doors," she told me. "All eyes are on you. You're not an ordinary student. You're the face of this program. You can't be seen doing that."

I just sat there and listened, the thoughts echoing in my head: *Am I doing something wrong? Is that what Kim is trying to say?* That day at practice, some of my straight teammates (I wasn't the only gay player on the squad) were talking about the nice dinners they had with their boyfriends the night before. But none of them got called into Kim's office. And none of them had to answer for going to the movies with their significant others, the way I did when someone e-mailed Kim to say I kissed my girlfriend inside the theater during a midnight show. This anonymous person was upset because supposedly there was a kid in there. Let me repeat: it was a midnight show. Shouldn't that kid be in bed? Also, it's not like I was slobbering all over my girlfriend. I said as much to Kim, and I think she believed me. But she just said the same thing she always said: "Keep it behind closed doors."

THAT WINTER, I MET SOME students who were gay, and they invited me to a meeting, while making it clear that if word got out about the meeting, we would get kicked out of the space. "What do you mean, kicked out?" I asked, because I was still clueless about Baylor's official policy regarding homosexuality.

"We're not allowed to get together to talk about this stuff," one of the students told me. I honestly thought he was being dramatic. I knew Baylor was a religious school, so I figured meetings among gay students were probably something people didn't want to publicize by plastering flyers all over the place. If I had actually known about the policy at the time, the secretive nature of the meeting would have made more sense to me. Anyway, I went with two of my teammates, and when the three of us walked in, I could tell that people were surprised and excited to see us. There were about twenty students in the room, and our presence seemed to validate what they were doing, give them hope that if athletes were on board, maybe they could change some things. We sat in the back and just listened as they talked about being openly gay at Baylor. The vibe wasn't "Fight the Power!" It was more about finding ways to be true to yourself while also being aware of your surroundings. My teammates and I didn't stay too long, maybe thirty minutes, because I was still in my little rebel stage at the time, and I remember wishing the conversation had more edge. My attitude was kind of like, "Screw this—I'm not going to be quiet about who I am."

It was only later that year, when I finally learned about Baylor's written stance on gays, that I fully appreciated what those students were trying to do, and the risk they were taking just by having that meeting. I also began to realize athletes had an extra layer of protection, although one that came with its own set of handcuffs. I was on my way to class one day when I saw that someone had written "Love Being Gay" across the Baylor University sign in front of the school's main entrance. *That is awesome*, I thought, and then took a picture of myself standing in front of it, smiling big. But when I showed the picture to a gay friend of mine later that day, her reaction wasn't what I expected. She looked concerned, and she told me a pro-gay group had tagged the campus overnight, spray-painting messages like "Love" and "Pride" on signs and posters. "BG, you have to delete that pic," she said. "You can't show it to anyone."

I was baffled. "Why not?" Then she mentioned the policy, and I said, "Whoa, wait . . . what?" So she spelled it out for me, and my confusion quickly turned to anger.

"Fuck that policy," I said. "What's the point of it anyway? Why have something on the books if you're going to look the other way when it comes to someone like me?"

Just so we're all clear, here is the human sexuality portion of the "sexual misconduct" policy as it appears in the Baylor student handbook: *"Baylor University welcomes all students into a safe and supportive environment in which to discuss and learn about a variety of issues, including those of human sexuality. The University affirms the biblical understanding of sexuality as a gift from God. Christian churches across the ages and around the world have affirmed purity in singleness and fidelity in marriage between a man and a woman as the biblical norm. Temptations to deviate from this norm include both heterosexual sex outside of marriage and homosexual behavior. It is thus expected that Baylor students will not participate in advocacy groups which promote understandings of sexuality that are contrary to biblical teaching. The University encourages students struggling with these issues to avail themselves of opportunities for serious, confidential discussion, and support through the Spiritual Life Office or through the Baylor University Counseling Center."*

Anyone paying attention knew that I'm gay, including the high-rolling alumni who supported our program and mingled with us. They had chatted up my girlfriend freshman year, when she was waiting for me after games: *How's Brittney? Does she like it here? We're so happy to have her at Baylor.* I didn't walk around campus holding hands with my girlfriend, but when we ran into each other on the way to class, I would give her a long hug or wrap my arm around her shoulder. My sexuality was an open secret—not a secret at all, really, except I was being told not to talk about it publicly, even though no one in a position of authority actually cited the policy to me. So, again, what is the point of the policy exactly? It seems like if you believe in something enough to actually write it down, then you should stand by it; otherwise, get rid of it.

The hypocrisy was hard to stomach. There is so much about Baylor that I love, especially the people I met there—gay people, straight people, all kinds of great people. It's not like I have some kind of vendetta against the school; that's not why I'm revealing the struggles I had there, how I felt silenced. I would love to be an ambassador for Baylor, to show my school pride, but it's hard to do that—it's hard to stand up and say, "Baylor is the best!"—when the administration has a written policy against homosexuality. I've spent too much of my life being made to feel like there was 115 something wrong with me. And no matter how much support I got as a basketball player at Baylor, it doesn't erase the pain I felt there. The more I think about it, the more I feel like the people who run the school want it both ways: they want to keep the policy, so they can keep selling themselves as a Christian university, but they are more than happy to benefit from the success of their gay athletes. That is, as long as those gay athletes don't talk about being gay.

I know Kim walked that line. She was always talking about the image of the program, worrying what people would think. She hates tattoos, just like my dad does. She would say she was concerned my tats might give people the "wrong impression" about me, and Baylor, so she made me wear a T-shirt under my uniform to cover them up. We argued about it a lot my senior year, when we were butting heads all the time, about everything. But when it came to my sexuality, and the sexuality of other gay players, it's hard to know how much of Kim's don't-ask-don't-tell policy was about coaching at Baylor and how much of it was about living inside the paranoid world of women's college basketball, where too many coaches spend an unhealthy amount of time worrying about whether their programs will be seen as "too gay."

All I know for sure is that I felt like I was carrying around a giant weight everywhere I went—a growing sense that who I am, at my very core, needed to be hidden away in order for me to survive my time at Baylor.

TOO MUCH RED BERRY

I spent a lot of my free time sophomore year the same way I spent it as a freshman: going out and partying. But there was something different fueling me now. My freshman year, I was enjoying the freedom of being away from home for the first time, the sense of adventure. My sophomore year, I was trying to escape the feeling that I wasn't free at all, that I was a muted version of myself. Although I stayed in Waco most weekends, I'm obviously easy to spot when I'm out in public, so I'm pretty sure that word of my, um, extracurricular activities got back to Kim. She would occasionally check in with me to ask how I was doing and if I was still seeing my therapist. She never specifically asked me about drinking or partying; she would just address it in her typical Kim way. "Gotta get your sleep, Big Girl," she'd say. "You can't produce if you don't sleep." Or she would talk to the whole team, but let her eyes linger a little bit longer on me. "It's the middle of a long season," she might say. "Y'all need to be taking care of your bodies. You can't be out late." I knew she was right. Just like I knew that drinking because I was mad or sad was only going to make me madder or sadder. What I didn't know was that I needed to feel worse before I could somehow start to feel better.

I needed a wake-up call.

Toward the end of sophomore year, there was a big Greek party at Baylor, the all-black party, where everyone was supposed to show up wearing nothing but black. The school year had started with the all-white party, but I never even made it to that one, because it was right around the same time I was going through my rocky breakup with my girlfriend from freshman year, and I ended up having too much to drink with my friends earlier in the night. Now everybody was talking about the all-black party, and I was amped for it. Basketball season was over (we had made it to the Elite Eight of the NCAA tournament), and I was more than ready to put sophomore year behind me.

A few of us went to the mall that day and bought fresh outfits: shoes, shirts, pants. Our game plan that night was to drink a little bit at my place, then go to another apartment where we would pregame before going to the actual party. (So my apartment was the pre-pregame party.) We bought a bottle of Ciroc Red Berry vodka, and we were drinking it straight up, either poured into cups or directly out of the bottle. Except I was drinking faster than everyone else, so I killed the bottle (with some help) before we even left for the second apartment.

I don't know who drove my car to the next apartment complex, but it sure wasn't me. As soon as I got out of the passenger seat, I realized I couldn't go into the apartment, because I could barely stand. I told my friends to go ahead, waving them on with a flick

118

of my wrist, promising I would be along in a few minutes. Then I sat down on the ground with my back against the car, while everything else around me was spinning. After a few minutes (or maybe it was longer, who knows?), I was really struggling to remain upright, so I slumped forward against the left front tire, which was turned sharply to the side—because whoever drove my car to the party was apparently in such a hurry to park, they turned the wheel while getting out. Now I was hugging that tire like a pillow, fading in and out of consciousness. I remember people walking past me to go upstairs, and hearing them stop and say, "Oh my God, Brittney! Are you okay? What's wrong?" I kept saying, "I'm fine! Go on!" (Imagine me slurring my words and drawing out the word *fine* in one long syllable.) I also remember looking down at my brand-new black shirt and seeing a big dirty tread mark on the front.

And then I threw up.

When my friends realized I had never made it inside the apartment, they came back for me, and I told them to take me home right away. I don't really remember the car ride; the next scene in my mind is when I was stumbling through my front door, then going down in a heap on the floor. My roommate, Patrick—we all called him Stitch—had to carry me to the couch. I was burning up. He brought me water, and I drank as much as I could, but my body was rebelling against what I had put inside it. I was throwing up, then going through those other awful stages: fever, sweats, chills. At one point, I almost asked Stitch to take me to the hospital, that's how miserable I was feeling. I was having trouble putting thoughts together, and I wasn't even sure I could talk, because my body was using so much energy to counter the effects of the alcohol. I remember lying on that couch, desperate, and realizing I had made myself this sick. I had done this to myself. There was no one else to blame.

When I woke up the next morning, I was embarrassed. (I also had a pounding headache and my body felt like it had been trampled by bulls.) There were a lot of things out of my control—my mother's health, my father's relentless judgments, Kim's way of handling things—but I had lost sight of the fact that how I chose to deal with it all was still very much in my control. No matter what anyone else said to me, no matter how much it all hurt me at times, I didn't have to let it define me. Before I had even gotten up off that couch, I made a vow to stop running from the pain and to start channeling my energy into becoming as strong off the court as I was on it. Of course, it is often in our lowest moments when we make these promises to ourselves. What matters much more is the work we do every day to make the promises a reality and to learn from the struggle.

I wasn't exactly sure how these changes would look. I just knew I wanted to make them.

120

UNFINISHED BUSINESS

Our perfect season started with a loss. On March 29, 2011, my sophomore season ended one game shy of the Final Four, when we lost to Texas A&M in the NCAA regional final in Dallas (yes, the team coached by Gary Blair, who had recruited me harder than anyone). We had already beat the Aggies three times that season; in fact, we had won eight games in a row against them. We had their number. Or so we thought. We were playing at American Airlines Center, and more than eleven thousand fans showed up. The place was loud, electric, the kind of stage you want for a big game. Except we didn't show up. We came out flat and stayed flat. We couldn't hit a shot to save our lives. We turned the ball over 20 times. I even missed a dunk. Nothing was working. We lost by 12 points, but it felt like we got blown out.

And that's exactly what we needed. After that loss, we had a come-to-Jesus meeting, just us players. The coaches had said all the usual things: "You have to put in the work and get serious about what we're trying to accomplish here." But we knew as players we needed to get closer on the court. We needed better chemistry. So we decided to spend more time bonding that summer. Workout sessions, pickup games—that's where it all started. We also asked our strength and conditioning coach to arrange an outing one afternoon. There's an outdoor adventure area near campus, and it has a ropes course, one of those group challenge activities that help develop trust and teamwork. Each of us had to climb to the top of a telephone pole, then jump off to grab a bar a few feet away. We went in pairs and wore safety harnesses attached to a rope held by the team. If you jumped and missed the bar, everybody steadied the rope to keep you hanging in the air, so you didn't fall to the ground. But even with the harness, it's scary as hell—not just for the jumper, but also for everyone holding the rope. I know I did not want to jump. No way. I didn't want to trust everybody, my life hanging in the balance. *Coming up on News at 11: Baylor center Brittney Griner fell and broke her head today. We have the shocking details!* But I did what I had to do. I was paired with Jordan Madden, another junior, and we both jumped and grabbed the bar. My long arms came in handy. Phew.

We also did a group exercise down by the marina, on the Brazos River, where I would often go kayaking. We had to build makeshift rafts out of whatever material was available—inner tubes, empty barrels, PVC pipes, rope, duct tape. Then we had to float around for a while on the river and make it back without sinking. We were split into two groups, and the other team's raft sunk, which gave us all a good laugh. It might sound obvious, but

122

those activities reminded us of an important lesson: everybody on a team has a job to do. And every job, big or small, is tied to a larger mission. The key is learning how to share the burden and find the right balance. That summer, we came together as a team. We would work out hard in the weight room, then go hard again in pickup. Everybody was putting in the extra effort to get better.

For me, that effort wasn't just about basketball. I knew I needed to grow up off the court. As a sophomore, I scored 23 points a game and was a first-team All-American, but I made things a lot harder on myself with all the partying and worrying about things that were out of my control. So I told myself, going into junior year, I wanted to have my shit together. That meant staying in more often, drinking less, keeping a tighter circle. If I wasn't kicking back with a few friends at House 4106—the place I shared with my teammate and good friend Shanay Washington—you could probably find me at House 41, the big red house, chilling with the bros. I had met Julio Trejo at a baseball game the previous spring, through mutual friends. We struck up a conversation during the game, and he happened to mention his birthday was in a few days. So I sent him a picture of myself on his big day, with the message "Happy Birthday, Princess!" He thought it was funny, and we've been close friends ever since. Julio lived at House 41 in Aspen Heights, off campus, with Nash Ingram and two other guys, and we all clicked hard from the start. Julio and Nash were big fans of Baylor sports, but they were also really down-to-earth guys who let me be myself. We played video games—*Modern Warfare, Madden, Assassin's Creed*—listened to music, barbecued, rode our longboards, and just hung out. As soon as I got out of class or practice, I headed for House 41. Sometimes I crashed there. I guess you could say I was leaning on those guys for support, without even thinking about it. We were just there for each other every day, kind of like holding the ropes. I'm not saying we acted like adults all the time; we still did some stupid things. But I felt like I had more routine in my life off the court. I wasn't bouncing from one place to the next, one party to another party, or sitting around feeling angry at the world. Spending time at House 41 was a much better way to unwind and have fun than just following the crowd, getting wasted, and waking up with tire marks on my shirt.

BY THE TIME BASKETBALL SEASON started, our team was locked in. It was scary how good we were right from the beginning. Kim always schedules tough nonconference teams, so we had a chance to test ourselves early on. We beat Notre Dame and Tennessee in November, then Connecticut in December. And when the Big 12 season got going in January, we were rolling through teams, blowing them out by 30 points a game. We had a close game at Texas Tech in mid-January, when we won 72–64, and then we crushed our next eight opponents. It was during that stretch when we started saying to each other, "Damn, we could go undefeated in conference." That is a hard thing to do in a league as strong as the Big 12, which is known for hard-nosed defense, low-scoring games, and loud crowds. The Big 12 always leads the nation in attendance for women's basketball. Fans come out to support their schools, especially against us, and we were going into opposing arenas and making good teams look bad.

Our goal entering the season was to win the national championship. We had four starters returning, and we were No. 1 in the preseason polls. So we were focused on going undefeated when it mattered most, in the NCAA tournament. Win six games, and you win it all. But we were so dominant in the Big 12, we started talking about it among ourselves, that maybe we could run the table and go 40-0, something no team had ever done in college basketball. A few other schools had gone undefeated in the past—Texas, Tennessee, and Connecticut—but no team had won 40 games in a season. When reporters asked us about it, we deflected the questions and said the usual things about wanting to win the Big 12 title, the Big 12 tourney, and the NCAA championship. In private, though, the idea of going undefeated gave us extra motivation as we got deeper into the season.

You could see it with the coaches, too. They tried to crack down on us more. Kim was all about us being a unit. She wanted us wearing the same color shoes, the same color socks, the same practice outfits. She was really anal about it and kept telling us, "I'm not letting anything go this season. I relaxed on y'all last season, but we're going to do this right. Everybody is going to buy into it." We would laugh about some of that stuff as players. I mean, why does it matter if I have on white socks and someone else has on black socks? Most of us were thinking, *Okay, Kim, whatever you say.* But one thing we could all agree on, coaches and players alike, was that we had unfinished business. That was our motto all season. We even made a video that we played on the big screen in the Ferrell Center before our home games. In the video, Kim is talking to us in the locker room, preaching about the dedication and hard work that goes into winning a national championship, reminding us of how we felt when we came up short the previous season. We knew we were more talented than most teams; what clicked for us was how much better we could be as a team if we each took care of our own business.

You could really see it that season with Odyssey Sims, our sophomore point guard. My recruiting class had been the best in the country when we showed up at Baylor, but like anybody making the transition from high school to college, we all had a lot to learn. And Odyssey was no different when she joined our team the following year. She brought a lot of effort and intensity to our games, but practice was a different story. She had mental lapses, some issues with how she handled criticism from the coaches, just

125

like I did as a freshman. It's an adjustment when you're used to having a lot of success doing things a certain way as a player, and then you find yourself constantly being scrutinized and called out by a big-time college coach who says, "You will do it my way now." I imagine that was especially tricky for Odyssey—aka "O"—because she played the same position Kim did in college. They're both feisty, strong-willed point guards who like to run the show. But we could see things click better for O her sophomore season. She was executing at a higher level on offense, which made her even more focused on defense. You hear people say about football players, "He has a nose for the ball." Well, O has a whole face for the ball. You won't find too many players who work harder on defense than she does. A lot of what we were able to accomplish defensively started with her, because she set the tone up top, pressuring the opposing point guard full court, making it harder for the other team to set up its offense and get the ball to the wings. And obviously they had to deal with me in the middle. As much as O loves stealing the ball, I love blocking shots. That's a good combination right there.

Coaches are always looking for different ways to motivate players. When a team is struggling, you have to push one set of buttons, to help the players get some confidence back. When a team is steamrolling everybody, you have to push a different set of buttons, to keep the players from being overconfident. There's no question Kim pushed a lot of the right buttons with our team that season. But she didn't always push the right buttons with me. Or maybe the way she went about it reminded me too much of my father. I just know that the push-pull with me and Kim started to get under my skin more during my junior year. And when I think about our run through the NCAA tournament, the game that stands out the most is the one against Tennessee in the Elite Eight, because Kim and I had one of those button-pushing moments.

Most people remember that matchup as Pat Summitt's last game. She had announced going into the season that she'd been diagnosed with Alzheimer's disease, so everyone was wondering if the NCAA tourney was her last run as Tennessee's coach. At the time, of course, we weren't thinking about that as players; all that mattered was that Tennessee stood between us and a trip to the Final Four. And from what I know about Coach Summitt, she wouldn't have wanted us looking at it any other way, because her teams always competed hard. They were known for their defensive intensity, and that's how we'd been winning all season—just shutting people down.

Women's basketball fans probably remember something else about that game: I got tossed out. It happened toward the end, when the outcome had already been decided. (We won 77–58.) I was on the bench with Jordan Madden and Terran Condrey, one of our seniors, and there was a little altercation out on the court. Odyssey got tangled up with one of Tennessee's players, and she landed on the floor in a vulnerable spot. The two of them started jawing at each other, so we walked onto the court—Jordan and Terran and me—to keep O from getting into any trouble. It's not like we ran out there looking to fight. When you watch the replay, you can see us hesitate a little; we were just trying to make sure everybody kept their cool. But the NCAA has a rule against leaving the bench, so the three of us got ejected. And Kim was so livid. Right before we got tossed, the refs were looking at the replay, to make sure they got everything right, and Kim went off on us. She was throwing her hands in the air, yelling at us: "That's the stupidest thing y'all did! You're probably done now! They're not gonna let you play the next game!"

That pissed me off. I know she was worried we might get suspended for the next game, at the Final Four, but it was clear we were trying to keep the peace, and the refs could see that on the

127

monitor. They did everything by the book. (Well, except they somehow missed that two Tennessee players had also left the bench.) We didn't get suspended because none of us went out there fighting. But the refs had to eject us for leaving the bench, which meant we had to walk to the locker room and wait for the game to end before we could come back out on the floor to cut down the nets and celebrate advancing to the Final Four. As you might imagine, that put a damper on things for me. It's not like I could just run back out on the court and be all happy. And Kim knew it. I was standing there at one point, several feet away from her, while everyone else was whooping it up, and she looked at me and pointed to her cheeks, signaling for me to smile. I just turned my head away from her.

When we all got back to the locker room, she came up to me and said, "You know I had to do that." She told me she had to yell at us on the court to prove a point. She was always doing that, getting on me in front of everybody and saying, "This team is bigger than Brittney Griner." But then in private, she would tell me, "I'm not really mad at you, Big Girl. You know how much we need you." Um, okay. Then what is the point of that exactly? It was all for show? Sometimes I would get in trouble for passing the ball too much. Kim made such a big deal about running the offense through me—and sure, I know my height caused a lot of problems for teams. But I didn't want anybody thinking I had to have the ball all the time for us to win. And I certainly didn't need to be reminded that the team was bigger than me. We were all pieces that fit together. So why call me out in front of my teammates if you're just going to take me aside afterward and downplay the whole thing? Kim has a lot of qualities that I respect, but I can't stand all that business about putting on a public front. I would understand if she got mad at me for something and stayed mad. That happened, no doubt. It was the

128

mixed messages that made it hard for me to know where she was coming from sometimes.

Maybe that had something to do with everything that was happening off the court. Maybe she worried more about my mind-set than I thought she did. I really don't know. During a big media session at the Final Four in Denver, the day before we played Notre Dame for the national championship, a reporter asked Kim about all the awful things people said about me on social media and the taunts I heard when we played on the road. It was an interesting moment, for a few different reasons. Up until that point, there hadn't been much public acknowledgment of all the trolling, all the ugly comments. People are always attacking women's sports, especially women's basketball, calling us inferior, comparing us to men, trying to knock us down—all the sexist garbage that women face every day in society. I learned in college that you can't dwell on it, because the stronger we get, the more threatening we are to those small-minded people. But sometimes it feels like people within women's sports don't want to talk about it in public. They just want to put a happy, smiley face on everything (*look how far we've come!*), as if ignoring the sexism and the racism and the homophobia will somehow make it less of a problem. The more that I was in the spotlight, the harder it became for people involved in women's hoops—players, coaches, fans, media—to pretend that this dark cloud didn't exist. And to Kim's credit, she didn't sidestep it that day. You could hear the passion in her voice when she answered that question and defended me. She was Kim the protective mom, reminding everyone that I'm a real person with real feelings. She said, "This child is as precious as they come," and that she loved going to work and seeing my face, because I made her happy.

That last part made me laugh a little, because there were plenty of days I did not make Kim happy, and vice versa. We both have

129

a flair for the dramatic, which is another reason I remember that media session in Denver. Don't get me wrong: I believe Kim meant what she said on that podium. It wasn't just for show. But at the same time, it reminded me of all that was left unsaid. We could acknowledge, in a general way, that people were questioning my gender, calling me a freak, a man, a female imposter. And yet I couldn't talk about being gay. Most of the time, I was on autopilot with the media, because I couldn't really show who I was off the court, not the whole picture. The way I was often portrayed—just a big, fun-loving, goofy kid—felt like a two-dimensional version of the real me.

When we beat Notre Dame to win the title, I celebrated by making "snow angels" in the confetti on the court. There was so much paper, I couldn't resist dropping down like a kid in the snow. That was pure joy right there, but also a huge release. For one thing, the previous forty-eight hours had been draining, both mentally and physically. You don't necessarily feel that way when it's all happening, but it hits you afterward. I'll admit, during the first half of our semifinal game against Stanford, I was worried we might lose. We were sluggish and out of sync, and they played great defense the whole game, especially on me and Odyssey. Thank God for Terran Condrey, who gave us a huge spark off the bench. She made some big shots early in the second half, and really showed what kind of depth we had as a team. That game was a grind. And as soon as we won, our attention shifted to Notre Dame. Even though we had faced them early in the season, I acted like I knew nothing about their players and needed to watch as much video of them as I could. I felt like I was cramming for an exam, and that DVD was my textbook. I studied their big girl, Devereaux Peters, so much that I saw her in my sleep. She was a high-energy player, just really active around the basket, so I knew I needed to box her out and try to get her in foul trouble (which I did).

I also studied Skylar Diggins, their point guard. She was maybe the only guard in college who could get a floater off over me. She had figured it out in previous games—releasing the ball very quick—so I had to change my footwork and take an extra step to go up and try to block or alter her shot. At one point, I was sitting in my room watching clips, and I texted Odyssey and said, "Hey, we gotta get this thing done." She wrote back, "We gonna get it. We gonna get it."

And we did. We pulled away in the second half and won big over Notre Dame. On a personal level, it was special because that was the first real championship I had ever won—not just a conference title, but the first time I had finished a season with a win. Also, I already had been named national Player of the Year that season, so lifting a championship trophy made all the individual awards so much more special. Most of all, winning the national title meant we had accomplished what we had set out to do as a team, and what my class had talked about doing when we all committed to Baylor. We finished our business. And for all the doubts I had earlier in my college career, all the frustration and emotional struggles, I never stopped wanting to bring a championship to Waco, because the campus and the community always supported our team. We also knew how much it meant to Kim, to get that second ring. A lot of people were surprised when Baylor won the national championship in 2005, but everyone expected us to win this time around. And even though we turned that pressure into fuel, it still took its toll. Kim was diagnosed with Bell's palsy the week before the Final Four. Her facial nerves were messed up. One side of her face was droopy (she couldn't smile), her hearing was bothering her, and her eyes were really sensitive. She had to wear sunglasses during some of her interviews, which made her look like a celebrity recluse. She joked about it with the media, but it was a visible reminder for everybody, the stress on her face.

131

Looking back now, I wish I could have stayed on that court longer, making those confetti angels, wiping away all the hard stuff I had dealt with—just enjoying the moment as long as possible. Because once we got back to Waco, there wasn't much time for me to exhale before all the pressure and all the expectations started building again. There had been a lot of speculation at the Final Four that I might leave Baylor after my junior year and go pro early. I shot that down in Denver and made it clear I wanted to finish college. You can't relive those four years of your life, and I was looking forward to my senior year.

Little did I know it would be so challenging.

ADVENTURES IN LONGBOARDING

Life was pretty crazy for a while after we won the NCAA championship. Good but crazy. I couldn't really go anywhere in Waco because people acted like it was the first time they'd ever seen me in person; everybody wanted to stop and say hi or take a picture. When I was a little kid, I loved people. My parents say I used to hug everyone I met. I still love people, most of the time. But Waco is a small place, and it's not like I blend in when I'm out in public. Just going to class was a challenge. And if I needed something at the store, I would ask somebody to get it for me. That was kind of a drag. I had never imagined myself as being any kind of celebrity. It's one thing to deal with the media during March Madness, when the spotlight is on us as players, but the level of attention after we got back on campus was pretty intense.

At the same time, though, I was on such a high. I was finally getting a chance to enjoy the ride. And being Brittney Griner definitely had its advantages in Waco. A few weeks after we won the title, I was out with my boys late one night—Nash, his housemate Albert, our friends A.J. and Mikey—and I had the bright idea of longboarding while holding on to the back of Mikey's car. "We are real skaters," I said to them. "Let's just do this and have some fun." Those guys didn't need any convincing. So I grabbed the spoiler on Mikey's Mitsubishi Lancer, along with Mikey, Nash, and Albert; then A.J. got behind the wheel and started driving. We rode around the whole campus like that, cruising down Main Street, University Drive, probably hitting 30 or 40 miles per hour, which feels pretty damn fast when you're on a board. It was like that scene in *Back to the Future 2,* when Michael J. Fox is on his hoverboard, riding behind the car—just an insane rush. I think we were so focused on what we were doing, we didn't even think about anybody seeing us. When we got to the Ferrell Center, we slowed down and decided to head home. It was around 1 A.M. at that point, and we were only a few seconds away from hopping off our boards.

Of course, that's when I spotted a campus police car sitting in the Ferrell parking lot. I said, "Y'all, that's a cop over there. Are we gonna stay and let him pull us over, or are we gonna dip?" We knew the guy had probably seen us; it would have been hard to miss us unless he was snoozing. Sure enough, before we even had time to react, he was already coming toward us. Then he threw on his lights and pulled us over. We all got off our boards and just stood there, waiting like a bunch of little kids who got caught running in the halls at school. I was wearing a pair of ripped jean shorts, my Vans, and a sports bra, no shirt, and I wedged myself in behind the bros, hunching over and lowering my eyes. I had one

134

thought in my head: *Fuuuuck!* The officer didn't see me at first. I think he thought I was one of the dudes. He walked up and said, "Whatcha guys doing?" But we didn't say anything because we could tell he was pissed. He looked at us for a few seconds, then said, "This is the most boneheaded thing I've seen in a long time. What the heck are y'all thinking?" He paused and shook his head. "I need to see some identification from everybody."

I had to lift my head when I gave him my license. He squinted a little to read it, and then his eyes got wide. He looked up at me and said, "And you? Does Coach know you're out here?"

That is one of the more comical questions I've ever heard, now that I think about it. "Well, sir, she knows I like to longboard," I said, all sheepish-like. "She just doesn't know how I do it exactly."

He shook his head again and said, "You just won a national championship, and this is what you're doing?" He didn't even check the other IDs after that. All he said was, "Put the boards in the back, get in the car, and go home." I had been pretty nervous up until that point, because when he told us how boneheaded we were being, that's when it finally hit me, like, *Oh yeah, that was a really stupid thing we did.* But as soon as he let us off the hook, I felt this giant wave of relief. "Yes, sir," I said, trying to look as serious as possible, while in my head I was like, *Hell yes!* And then he said, "Y'all get the gold star for the night—for the month, actually." That's when I had to bite my lip to keep from laughing. I mean, what we did was reckless. DO NOT TRY THIS AT HOME. But the fact that we were dumb enough to do it, and that we walked away without getting hurt and without getting in trouble? I couldn't help cracking up about it afterward, at the absurdity of it all. The guys kept saying, "Damn, we're glad you were with us, B, because we would have been toast otherwise." It's like they had forgotten that I was the one who had the crazy idea in the first place.

135

I WOULD EVENTUALLY pay the price for pushing the limits on my longboard. And everyone would find out about it. We rode a lot that spring, me and the boys, for hours at a time. We liked to hit the parking garages around campus—take the elevator up, then ride down. Nothing too crazy. But one day in early May, a couple of weeks after our late-night stunt with Mikey's car, the fun came to an end. There is one particular spot, in the bookstore parking garage, that's more challenging. The ramp to go up is really steep, which means you pick up more speed on the way down. Naturally, we decided to ride it. Mikey went down first and barely made it around the first turn at the top. I thought about it for a few seconds and said, "Okay, I can do it." But I walked halfway down the ramp first, so I could start from the middle and keep my speed under control. Unfortunately, that didn't help. Almost as soon as I got going, I could tell I was heading for a nasty spill if I tried to swing that turn. I shouted, "I'm not gonna make it!" And then I jumped off the board. But I was going so fast, I couldn't stop running. I must have looked like a cartoon character, just a big blur of arms and legs. I almost went headfirst into the curb, but I somehow managed to stay on my feet and threw my hands up to brace myself as I ran into the wall. My right hand—my shooting hand—absorbed most of the impact, and my wrist bent back at an awkward angle.

I knew right away something was wrong. It hurt like hell. I dropped down to the ground, holding my wrist, yelling and cussing. I said to the guys, "We have to go back to the car." So we all got on our boards—I wasn't thinking too clearly, obviously—and when we started to go, I said, "I can't do it. I just can't." I took my shirt off and wrapped it around my wrist to keep it still. The pain was getting worse by the second. Then I told the guys, "Y'all go get the car and pick me up. Grab my phone, call the trainer."

At first we couldn't get in touch with anyone because Kim was

136

attending an awards banquet in New York City and most of the staff was gone. But one of our assistant coaches, Rekha Patterson, was around, and she met us at the hospital. Julio and Nash waited with me. The x-rays confirmed what I already knew: my wrist was broken. I also knew I had to call Kim. Rekha had already told her, but I still had to check in. And I was dreading it. I thought Kim was going to rip me. Hell, I probably would have ripped me. I made sure I took my pain medicine before I called her, so at least I would be drowsy in case she started going off on me. But she didn't do that at all. She just said, "Big Girl, I hear you broke your wrist." She was sympathetic. Of course, she also said, "You know, if this had happened during the season, you would have hurt your team, too. I'm glad you have plenty of time to heal and rehab it. Do whatever you need to do to get better."

There wasn't much I could say, except, "I know, Coach. You're right. I'm sorry." It's not like Kim was going to ban me from riding, especially during the off-season. She's a demanding coach, but she didn't try to micromanage our every move off the court. We had a parade in Waco after we got back from the Final Four, and I rode my longboard in it. Kim trusted me to use my judgment when it came to riding, and I usually did. I just got a little carried away that spring, probably because I didn't have to worry about basketball. It was like I had a temporary free pass: I knew it wouldn't last, so I was just trying to have fun and not worry about what might come next. I knew I was lucky when I found out I wouldn't need surgery, just a cast for a month or so. Once I started rehab and worked through the stiffness, it didn't take long to get my shooting touch back.

If anything, the worst part of rehab was being stuck on the sidelines during our basketball camps for kids. I couldn't really do anything except show up and smile. And when it came time for the final send-off, well, that hurt a lot more than you might imagine. On the last day of each session, we always sign autographs. There's a line of kids (along with their sisters and brothers and moms and dads) that snakes around the gym and out the door—hundreds and hundreds of people—and we sit there signing and taking pictures for hours. I usually love signing for kids, but trying to do it with a soft cast on, holding the marker in an awkward way, was challenging to say the least. When I think about breaking my wrist, one of the first things that comes to mind is how much it hurt to sign those autographs. Ha. I'm pretty sure that's not what Kim was worried about when she reminded me I had to think about the big picture.

THE MOST IMPORTANT DECISION I faced after we won the championship was whether I wanted to play in the 2012 Summer Olympics in London. I had played for the U.S. national team the previous September, during a two-week training tour in Europe. I was the only college player on the squad, which was coached by Connecticut's Geno Auriemma, so I had a chance to hoop with a bunch of WNBA stars, including Cappie Pondexter, Tina Charles, and Swin Cash. And in February of my junior season, just two months before we won the NCAA title, I was named a finalist for the Olympic team, which was an incredible honor. I felt a lot of pride wearing that USA jersey during the European tour. The U.S. women had won four straight gold medals in basketball, and playing in the Olympics is something I had dreamed about since high school.

But I was exhausted after the season. Going 40-0 is hard enough, and it feels even harder when you have people pounding on you, hanging on you, knocking you around every single game. I knew if I played in the Olympics—if Coach Auriemma and USA Basketball decided to pick me—that by the time I got back from London in mid-August, I would have to jump right back into pre-

138

season training with Baylor. I was deep down tired. I also had other concerns weighing on me, mainly that I didn't want to be so far away from my mom. I had one year of college left, only a certain amount of time left in Texas, when I could see her mostly whenever I wanted. I knew that after I left Baylor and turned pro, I would see her a lot less, because it's hard for her to travel; it just takes so much out of her. And I worry about her all the time. Just having her close by, knowing she was only three hours away, gave me peace of mind. School was also a consideration. It had never been my first priority, but that just meant I needed to take care of business during summer classes, so I could stay on track and keep out of Kim's doghouse (where I would end up anyway at the beginning of my senior year).

One day in April, about a month before I broke my wrist, I was chilling with Julio and Nash, and I just put it out there: "Yo, guys, I don't think I'm going to do the Olympics." I had been thinking about it for a few days, and that was the first time I said it out loud. I told them I was tired, and Julio said, "Hell, yeah, you're tired. You need to rest and get off your legs." Then Nash said, "You'll have other chances to play in the Olympics." Those guys always give me honest feedback; they don't just tell me what they think I want to hear. If they had said, "Girl, you're crazy—this is a once-in-a-lifetime opportunity," I would have considered that carefully. But once I got their feedback, once I knew I wasn't being crazy, I talked to my parents about it, and they were cool with it, too. As always, my mom just wanted me to be happy. And I think my dad liked the idea of me being in Waco instead of London. He probably figured it would be easier to keep tabs on me.

When I told Kim I didn't want to go, she kind of already knew. She had been telling me all along, for a couple of months, "This is going to be a hard decision, so think it over real good." She never tried to sway me one way or the other; she was really cool about

139

staying neutral. I think early on, when I was named a finalist, she wanted me to go. She always said it was one of the best things she ever did, playing for the United States and winning a gold medal at the 1984 Summer Olympics. But she knew I was tired at the end of the season, and that I keep going and going until my body crashes. She knows I have trouble saying no, so she told me a few times, in the days leading up to my decision, "I know you don't want to let anybody down, but you need your rest, too. You had a long season." I think she knew by then which way I was leaning, so she wanted to make sure I knew it was okay if I didn't go, that she wouldn't be disappointed.

I was kind of hoping, when I walked into Kim's office to tell her, that she would break the news to the people at USA Basketball. I wanted to avoid that phone call. But Kim said, "You have to be a big girl about it and call them yourself." And then she made me do it right then and there, because she knew if I went home I probably wouldn't do it. (Sometimes I avoid saying no by not saying anything at all.) So I called Carol Callan, the women's national team director for USA Basketball. By that point, there was only one roster spot still open, and the general assumption was that they were holding it for me. I told Carol I was taking my name out of the equation, and she was very understanding. One of the things a lot of people didn't seem to realize—all those online trolls and people on message boards who would question my decision—was that I would have been the first college player since 1988 to make the U.S. team, which tells you something about how hard it is to play on that level. Some of the key players on the 2012 team were in their thirties: Diana Taurasi, Sue Bird, Tamika Catchings, Lindsay Whalen, Swin Cash. So it's not like the fate of the U.S. squad was resting on my shoulders. If that had been the case, I would have been there in a heartbeat, doing everything I could to bring home another gold.

Instead, my decision to stay in Waco fueled all these crazy conspiracy theories about me—how I'm secretly a man, and I wanted to avoid genetic testing at the Olympics. It's one thing to have people question my heart, although I don't know how anyone could do that after the season I had. But when they question my very being, my gender, and accuse me of living a giant lie, I can't even begin to understand that kind of ignorance and hate. And fear. It's sad, really, that there are so many people who are threatened by anyone who seems different, anyone who stands out because of how they look or act. I think most of the crap that people say about me is just a way to devalue my accomplishments. But I also think there are some paranoid, twisted fools out there who actually believe the accusations they make.

I have every intention of playing for the United States at the 2016 Summer Olympics in Brazil, if I'm selected for the team. And if some country wants to issue a challenge, bring it on. I don't have anything to hide. I'll do whatever I need to do, prove whatever point I need to prove, so I can play. And then maybe everyone will finally shut up.

But I doubt it. Some people will always find reasons to spout their nonsense. I've heard it my whole life, and it hasn't stopped me from being me.

THE FACE OF THE PROGRAM

I can't swim. I mean, I can swim a little, but it's not pretty. The thing is, I love the water. I love standing in the ocean or kayaking on a river or lake. I just get nervous if somebody starts messing with me, like grabbing my arm or my shorts. If I have a life jacket on, we can play all day, because I know if someone pulls me under, I'm coming back up. I had an uncle who drowned before I was born—my father's brother died when they were kids—so swimming wasn't something I did when I was young. That's probably why I'm like a big kid now when I'm in the water. I like it, but I'm also a little scared of it.

My senior season at Baylor started on the water, when we went to Hawaii for the Rainbow Wahine Classic. Although I didn't know it at the time, that trip would set the tone for my entire senior year, because I ended up feeling like I was swimming through it all. My teammates and I thought we were setting out to win another national championship. We had our core group back for another year, and we were telling each other, "It's going to be a great season. We're going out with a bang." We did some cool stuff during our trip to Honolulu, including a visit to Pearl Harbor, which I was really into because of my interest in military history. The last excursion that Kim planned for us was a snorkeling adventure the day before the opening game of the tournament. It was a lot of fun, even if there were a few times when I thought I might drown. But I'm sure Kim was regretting it afterward, because all that kicking took something out of us going into our game against Stanford.

Not that I'm making excuses. We lost that game for two reasons: (1) Odyssey Sims, our point guard, strained her hamstring in the first five minutes and missed the rest of the game, and (2) we were bigheaded, as if all we needed to do was show up and we'd win. During pregame warm-ups, we were down on our end of the court, cracking jokes. We were watching the Stanford players and making fun of them because they looked so serious. Somebody said, "They're going to tire themselves out before the game even starts," and we all laughed. But once the game actually did start, Stanford was on point. They were ready. And after O hurt her hamstring, we found ourselves in a big hole. It had been a long time since anybody had really challenged us. We'd won 42 games in a row, including two easy victories to open the season. Even when O left the Stanford game, we told ourselves, "It's early. We'll be okay." We actually did rally—the game was back and forth down the stretch—but we lost by two points, which put a cloud over the whole trip. After working so hard the previous season and making history by going 40-0, we flew to Hawaii and failed our first big test of the new season.

144

We were a little shell-shocked in the locker room after the game. Kim came in and said, "We had all this fun, we took you to all these places, and you didn't come out and play well." It felt like maybe we had ruined it for the next Baylor team that would travel somewhere exotic. I pictured Kim keeping everyone locked in the hotel, watching game film. That night, a bunch of us snuck out of our rooms and took a walk along the beach, trying to process what had happened. We all kept saying we couldn't believe we had lost that damn game. We told ourselves we couldn't lose again; we had to get it together. But there was a strange energy around us for the rest of the trip, because we didn't quite know how to act. Kim was clearly upset with us, and even though we steamrolled our next two opponents, they were so outmatched that beating them didn't exactly redeem us after the Stanford loss.

In the weeks to come, we would put a mental asterisk next to that loss, because Odyssey had missed most of the game. We pumped ourselves back up, believing no other team could beat us if we had all our pieces in place. In some ways, this attitude served us well, because we developed a knack that season for rallying in the second half of games. No matter how sluggish we would play in the first half, we'd come out of the locker room for the second half and tell ourselves, "Okay, now it's time to turn things around." But in other ways, our greatest strength was also our worst weakness. We were a strong-willed bunch, and Coach Mulkey had tapped into that the season before, pushing us to reach our full potential. Now she was determined to crack down on us again, because we had a talented group of freshmen on the roster, and Kim said she didn't want to make the same mistakes with them that she had made with us. She was nervous they would mimic our bad habits.

My classmates and I all marched to the beat of a different drummer. When we came together, we packed a powerful punch, but you could never quite predict when everyone would be on the same page. For example, during my first two seasons at Baylor, when we showed up at our shootaround on the morning of a game, we were all usually mismatched. Everyone was in Baylor gear, but some of us would be wearing our sweatpants, some of us our crinkly travel gear, some of us our practice jerseys—or a combination of everything. Starting my junior year, Kim made a bigger deal of it, and she would get mad if we didn't match. She tried to argue that it was easier to come together if we started from the same place. "It's the small things," she'd say. After we won the national championship, those small things became even more important to her, and she tightened the reins. But you have to understand, we had been in Kim's cross hairs since day one. I came to Baylor as part of the top-ranked recruiting class in the country, along with Jordan Madden, Kimetria Hayden, Mariah Chandler, and Shanay Washington. And during our freshman year, both Destiny Williams and Brooklyn Pope transferred in from other schools, so they were part of our core group too. (Shanay became a student assistant after her career was cut short by a string of ACL injuries.) Sometimes a coach can afford to bring young players along slowly, but Kim had high hopes for us right from the start, and those expectations only grew after we made the Final Four my freshman season.

I'm sure there were more than a few times in my career when our coaching staff would sit in a room together and talk about what a handful we were. Coaches are always trying to enforce the message that the sins of one player are the sins of the whole team. My freshman year, when we all shared a suite in the dorm, one of us was late to practice one day (it wasn't me, honest), so Kim called us together and said the rest of us were responsible for our teammate's mistake. We tried to explain that we had knocked on her door before we left for the gym, but she hadn't answered, and the door was locked, so we assumed she wasn't there. None of that mattered to Kim. "You left your teammate behind," she told us, as if we'd abandoned a fallen soldier on the battlefield. That message—you're only as strong as your weakest link—clicked for us during our perfect season. But by the time the next fall rolled around, it was pretty clear we were itching to get out from under Kim's thumb, even as we talked about going out in style and winning another championship.

I spent much of my senior year struggling with the conflicting emotions of wanting my freedom from Baylor while also being scared to leave. I would get excited imagining my future as a pro, but then I'd get sad when I thought about saying good-bye to my friends in Waco. Everything I did, all the little everyday stuff, like heading home after practice to chill out or hang with the bros, took on more meaning. Of course, I kept those feelings to myself a lot, because I wanted to enjoy that time with my friends, not bring everybody down by getting all sentimental. I remember I was standing in the backyard of House 41 one day, tossing the football with Julio and Nash, and I must have had a faraway look in my eyes, because one of them stopped and asked me if I was doing okay. "Yeah," I said. "I'm just going to miss y'all so much."

In those moments, they would always promise to stick with me, tell me they'd visit me in Phoenix as much as they could. They insisted that our little family wasn't going to fall apart, even though they both had another year at Baylor after I left. And I wanted so much to believe them. I was just having a hard time thinking about starting over somewhere else.

I HAVE A LOT OF respect for Kim Mulkey, a lot of fond memories. Even if we all liked to complain about some of her quirks as a coach, she treated us fairly for the most part and didn't show favoritism. She cracked down on us when we slipped up, and she held everyone accountable for their mistakes, including the coaches. She also runs a very structured program, which was good for me. We had practice at the same time every afternoon, 1:30, for all four years I was there, so that was one less thing for us to worry about when it came to planning our schedules. (It helps that Baylor has great basketball facilities.) Kim was in control, even if occasionally our group of seniors liked to think we were. What I appreciated more, though, was how Kim interacted with us away from the court. I know there are some coaches who keep a wall up all the time, but she would let us come over to her house on the weekends, to hang out in the game room, swim in her pool, or just chill in comfortable surroundings. She would joke around with us, too. I didn't always get her jokes, but I liked that she tried to have a sense of humor around us. Most of all, she helped me out a lot when I was dealing with my parents, when I was frustrated with my dad or worried about my mom. It wasn't even so much what she said; it was just nice to have a place to go where I could get away from it all without actually leaving town. Her son, Kramer, was in high school at the time, and I went to some of his baseball games. Kim the mom seemed pretty cool.

I wouldn't say we had a falling-out. The friction between me and Kim was more of a gradual thing, just layer added upon layer. The more comfortable I became with myself, the more frustrated I was that we were still butting heads about the same stuff, because it felt like she always saw me a certain way. Kim liked to think she could read me; she swore she knew me inside and out. There were definitely plenty of times when I felt like she knew a good amount. But while she could read me on the surface, I'm not sure she ever truly comprehended how deep some of my struggles were. She would often call me into her office when she thought I was distracted by something, and as I lowered myself into the chair across from her, I'd think to myself, *She's fixing to get this right. She can tell I'm in a bad way.* But she was always wrong with what she thought the issue was, because she always thought it was the same thing: "girlfriend problems," as she put it.

"Big Girl, close the door," she would say, which is how I knew we were about to have Kim's version of a heart-to-heart conversation. I'd say, "All right, Coach," and gently shut the door. Then I'd wait to hear what version of "girl problems" she would drop on me. One time, she gave me a dead-serious look and asked, "Is it 'ex' problems?" I covered my mouth so she wouldn't see me swallowing a smile.

The first time she ever asked me that question, maybe early in my sophomore year, she sounded like she was speaking a foreign language and was worried about using the wrong words. But by senior year, she was an old pro at it, probably because she had asked me so many times. At one point early in my senior season, Kim called me into her office for a chat because she could tell I was struggling. Almost as soon as the Phoenix Mercury had landed the No. 1 pick in the WNBA Draft lottery, which took place at the end of September, my mind had been working overtime. There was always the chance that Phoenix could have traded the rights to that pick, but nobody really thought that would happen. So once I knew where my new life would unfold, the idea of leaving Baylor became much more real. It wasn't just some vague notion anymore, lingering out there on the horizon. I had a place: Phoenix. I had a team: the Mercury. I knew exactly how far I would be from Houston, from home: 1,175 miles. I was going to be moving away from everyone and everything I knew, from the friends who had embraced me and let me be myself. And now my insides were in knots every time I thought about it.

"Is something going on with you and your girlfriend?" Kim was sitting at her desk, looking at me, and I was trying not to roll my eyes.

149

"Actually, Coach, I don't have a girlfriend right now," I told her. "And it's not girlfriend problems." That was the truth. I had broken up with my girl in Atlanta, and I hadn't started dating Cherelle. I tried to explain that I had a lot on my mind, but I didn't really open up to Kim because I didn't think she "got" me the way my friends did. And, yes, maybe she would have understood me better if I had shared more with her, but there was always a little bit of a disconnect with us, because I never really knew if Kim fully accepted me for who I am.

Like I said, there isn't one specific moment I can point to and say, "That's where it all went wrong." But there was one common thread: I didn't like when Kim would show one face in public and a different face behind closed doors. She would call me into her office to tell me I had done something wrong—like when someone saw me kissing my girlfriend at the movies—but then she would shift the burden away from herself, trying to imply she was just the messenger and this wasn't how she personally felt. Those conversations caused me a lot of confusion, a lot of pain. Just once, I wanted her to stop worrying about what everyone else thought and stand by my side. Instead, she would express the "appropriate" level of concern when someone complained about something I had done, and then she would tell me, "Big Girl, I'm not saying I agree with them. I'm just reminding you to keep your business behind closed doors."

I'm sure Kim thought she was being fair. And I'm sure there are some players who would shrug it all off, because they understand the nature of the business, that coaches are always trying to please everyone—or at least it seemed that way with Kim. Trust me, I understand the pressure to please, the impulse to show different faces to different people. But when we're talking about something as fundamentally important as my identity, I'm not going to let other people tell me how I should act. I did a lot for the

Baylor program and helped raise visibility for the whole school. The idea that my sexuality might somehow hurt recruiting is ridiculous. I know Kim was in a tricky spot because of Baylor's policy on homosexuality—not that she ever admitted that to me—but don't tell me you're okay with the fact that I'm gay, and then once I get on campus you tell me to keep the gay part hidden away. I don't think Kim is homophobic, but I do think she was hypocritical when it came to me. She worried too much about what other people might think, and not enough about what I myself actually did think.

This theme repeated itself throughout my senior year, from one issue to the next. Our first big disagreement was about my course load. I had made up my mind to finish my degree gradually (I was a general studies major), chipping away at my credit requirements in the year or two after I left school. This is how a lot of men's basketball players and football players complete their degrees, because they've spent so much time focused on their sports during the year that they're always a few credits shy. That's where I found myself at the start of my senior year, a few credits behind pace to graduate, and I wasn't the kind of student who could just load up on classes and plow through it all. Graduating on time was not my main priority at that point, although earning my degree was important to me, mostly because it was so important to my mom, and I never want to let her down. But Kim had her own plan for how I would earn my degree. She wanted to overload my class schedule so I'd graduate on time, which would help keep her graduation rate really high (more than 90 percent). I had a meeting with her, and she made it clear to me that this was nonnegotiable.

"It's going to be too much," I told her. She shook her head and said I had to do it. But I know myself: when I have too much on my plate, I get stressed. Some people like a jam-packed schedule. Their attitude is, the busier, the better. Not me. I have trouble eating and I become irritable. A few weeks into my senior year, I went to my academic adviser and dropped a class. Kim was furious. I was breaking her graduation streak. At least, that's why I thought she was upset, and I told her as much. She said I was wrong, that she wanted me to have the security of a degree, and that was the only thing motivating her. She also said if I didn't graduate, she wouldn't retire my jersey. But all that meant to me was that she didn't really understand what makes me tick. I don't care about awards. I don't need hardware to motivate me. I care about hooping, and I care about winning.

When I was growing up, my future didn't even include college, never mind a college degree. So the fact that I'm so close to getting mine is a direct result of basketball. And I will get that degree, because it would be foolish if I didn't. But school and education aren't the same thing, and sitting inside a classroom has never been my favorite way to learn. When something interests me, I will spend hours immersed in the subject. At Baylor, I had a few professors whose teaching style struck a chord with me, because instead of just standing in front of the students and lecturing, or flipping through a PowerPoint presentation, they engaged us in a way that made the subject come to life, and everybody joined the conversation, like we were all part of a team. One of my history professors would put us into groups, and we learned about daily life in ancient Greece or medieval times by playing these games she created. We would act out the wars and battles; we bartered and loaned money. You might pull a card that said, "The Plague," and everybody in your town would die. It was interactive and fun, and I learned a lot more in that class than I did when some professor was just standing up and droning on the whole time.

As a kid, I was obsessed with the Animal Planet channel. I would sit there watching and learning about different species and subspecies, then I'd tell my parents all about it at the dinner table.

I would just talk, talk, talk, telling them stories about different animals. As I've gotten older, I've become more interested in black history and movies about the civil rights movement. My interests are all over the place. At one point during my first summer in Phoenix, I downloaded a bunch of books about Marilyn Monroe. I'm fascinated by her story, because she seemed to have had it all, and yet she was always searching for something else. In public, she was portrayed as the ideal woman, but it was a different story in private. She was so vulnerable.

Anyway, the point is, I was not the ideal student at Baylor. I had so much other stuff going on that I didn't always have the focus I needed for my classwork. I know I could have been more dedicated at times, but I felt like Kim thought I could just flip a switch my senior year and turn into Wonder Student—and that just wasn't going to happen.

Unfortunately, our battle over how many credits I should take wasn't our only clash of wills. Winning the 2012 national championship was amazing, but it also put a spotlight on the program that was even brighter than we expected, raising the stakes for Kim, for me, for all of us. And the more attention we got, the more Kim and I butted heads over another topic: my tattoos. It was clear from all the comments she made that she thinks tattoos send the wrong message, and she doesn't understand why anybody would ever get one. When I got my two star tats freshman year, front and center on each shoulder, I threw her for a loop because now her star player, the one grabbing all the headlines, seemed to be making some kind of statement Kim didn't understand. (The statement was this: "I love the way these stars look!") So she made me wear a T-shirt under my jersey and said she was doing me a favor, protecting me from the judgment of millions. She also warned me that if I kept getting tats, I would probably lose out on endorsement money.

In my eyes, this was a form of censorship and an old-fashioned way of looking at the world. My senior year, we would sit in Kim's office (yes, I spent a lot of time in there) and go around in circles about the whole tattoo issue. She said she knew I was angry with her for making me hide my tats. But that wasn't exactly true: I was upset because it seemed like all she cared about was the image of the program as seen through the eyes of a very specific segment of the population. I was upset because she believed people would label me a bad person simply because of my tattoos. I was upset because, once again, Kim was allowing other people—or, in this case, the fear of what they might say—to decide how she responded to me.

I'm not overlooking the pressure Kim felt when it came to maintaining the image of her program. I'm just saying I think she worried about the wrong things sometimes. It's not like we were all causing trouble off the court, bringing shame to the university, like the way some men's teams cause headaches for their schools. We were good members of the Baylor community, not a bunch of bad seeds. At one point that season, Brooklyn Pope, a starting forward for us, produced a music video of herself rapping, which was her passion outside of basketball. Apparently a parent of a recruit saw the video posted online and wrote a long note to Kim about how disappointed he was that she allowed Brooklyn to use those lyrics, to send a message that the parent didn't agree with. So Kim got on all of us about the video and told Brooklyn to take it down. We tried to stick up for Brooklyn, to reason with Kim. We said, "Brooklyn is a rapper, Coach, so of course her songs aren't going to sound like the country music you listen to, like Trace Adkins. But it's basically all the same. Brooklyn using the word 'ass' is no different than Trace singing about 'honky tonk badonkadonk' and staring at a woman's butt!"

As usual, Kim reminded us to keep it behind closed doors, the

154

same way she wanted me to cover up my tattoos. I told her I didn't want to be one of those athletes who worry so much about managing their public images that you never really know who they are on the inside. I know who I am, and if you get to know me, you know what's in my heart. So if people I don't know want to take one quick look at me, at my tattoos, and assume I'm a bad person—well, I don't care if they do. Why should I waste mental energy worrying about the negative opinions of people I've never met? I care a lot more about the people who know me. I care about the fans who don't know me personally but who respond to me positively. I also told Kim I didn't want to work with any company that didn't understand why I have tattoos. Endorsement deals are nice, but not at the expense of your personal truth.

I was walking along the hallway in the basketball offices one day when I noticed a photo, a framed action shot, of a former player who had a Mickey Mouse tattoo on her shoulder. There it was, in all its glory, out in the open during a game. The player in that photo had much darker skin than I do, so her tat didn't pop like mine do. But ink is ink, and I asked Kim straight up: "You've had other players with tattoos, so why is it such a big deal with me?"

"Big Girl, you're the face of the program," she said. "All these little girls look up to you, and I don't want their parents to think anything bad about you." In my mind, her answer translated two ways: first, that I should feel some sense of shame about my tattoos, and second, she didn't want anybody to have a bad opinion of the program because of how I look.

My senior year, I got a flower tattoo on my left shoulder. I also came up with a twisted solution to the whole tattoo issue, one that would satisfy both Kim and me. I wanted to wear a long-sleeve shirt under my jersey, because I was always getting scratched during games. But I was also going overboard to prove a point, like a little kid refusing to talk for hours after her parents ask her to be quiet for a few minutes. I knew Kim wouldn't want me to wear the long sleeves, because nobody else on the team wore them, and she was anal about us all having the same look. She couldn't really argue with me about the scratches, so she relented on the long-sleeve tee, with one condition: I had to agree not to get any more tattoos until I was done playing for Baylor. We also had to clear the uniform change with the NCAA, because you need a medical reason to wear long sleeves, so we said I was trying to keep my joints warm. (Can't play with cold joints, right?)

And, yes, I kept my promise to Kim. I didn't get another tattoo until I left Baylor.

156

HELLO AND GOODBYE

My dad and I had stitched together our relationship, kind of anyway, after I moved out, and then back home, during my senior year of high school. He came to all my games at Baylor. I did my part, too: I would usually answer his calls, and I'd tell him how many miles I put on the car. It was an uneasy peace, punctuated by lots of silly arguments. He was still in the habit of lecturing me, and although I usually just tuned him out, all his preaching was growing more tiresome. If, for example, a professional athlete did something particularly stupid or got into trouble with the law, my cell phone would buzz, and my dad was on the other end of the line, telling me all the ways in which I was at risk of suffering a downfall. If I had been at Baylor when Michael Vick was arrested for his role in dogfighting, that's exactly the kind of thing my dad would have gone off the rails about, warning me to watch my back. "Don't trust your so-called friends," he would say. "Everyone is out to get you, including the people you think you can count on. Keep your eye on them, on everyone. You can't trust your friends."

These calls weren't conversations. He wasn't checking in to ask how my day was going. He was talking at me, filling me with the pessimism and paranoia that constantly bubbled inside him. I received hundreds of these calls and texts during my career at Baylor, each one like a stone placed on top of the other, until this growing stack had become a wobbly leaning tower threatening to crash down on us. And the final piece, the one that made the whole thing topple, was a text he sent during my senior year.

When I was a kid, I never felt like I had anyone I could really confide in, someone who would listen carefully to me, someone who would understand my pain and anxiety, helping me to unburden my soul. I love my family so much, but who would fill that role for me? My dad? He was often the main reason I was upset. My mom? She hates confrontation; she wants everyone to get along. If I had tried to talk with her about my frustrations—especially how I felt suffocated by my dad's distrust of everyone—I would have put her in a no-win situation. Pier and I were too busy getting on each other's nerves, and DeCarlo and SheKera were so much older, they weren't plugged in to what I was doing, what I was feeling, day in and day out. I know DeCarlo would have understood a lot of it, because we had some talks in the backyard or in his truck and he would tell me to keep my chin up. But I was always so happy to see him, I didn't want to spend our time together talking about things that made me sad.

I know now how damaging it was for me to hold everything inside, because if you swallow all your resentments, they just simmer and fester until you explode. And that's exactly what happened

158

with me during my final year at Baylor: I blew my top, and the red-hot lava spilled all over my dad.

BY THE TIME I WAS a senior, the only control my father had over my life was the car, my trusty Dodge Magnum. He wasn't paying for college, he wasn't paying for my cell phone (Pier took care of that), and he wasn't giving me spending money because I had a small stipend with my scholarship. So everything came back to the car, and he started paying even closer attention to the miles I was putting on it. This obsession of his irked me more than usual because I wasn't driving all that much. I was probably using the car about the same amount as any typical Baylor student with wheels. One day in November, not long after the regular season had started, he sent me a text that was part lecture, part interrogation about the odometer on the car. There was nothing all that significant about what he said or how he said it—he was just being his usual Raymond Griner self—except this text happened to be the last stone placed on top of the tall, shaky pile. I stared at my phone as the anger rose inside me. I was twenty-two years old, and I wanted him to start treating me like an adult, instead of like a small child with no understanding of how the world works. I know my dad loves me. I know he would do almost anything for me (with emotional strings attached). But what I wanted most for him to do was nothing. I wanted him to release his grip on the reins of my life and allow me to make the mistakes we all make, so I could learn and grow without having to hear him say, "I told you so."

I realized right then and there, looking at my phone with growing outrage, that I needed to give him back the car. Those four wheels were the last strings connecting me to him, making me his puppet. And he was tugging those strings for all they were worth. I tried to call him because I felt this sudden urge to tell him off, to unload all the hurt that had been building inside me for so many

159

years. But he didn't answer. So I wrote him a text message, and then another, and another, and another, text after text after text, a stormy sea of green bubbles on my iPhone, maybe fifty texts in all—so many that it hurt my thumb to scroll through them. I probably sent him at least a thousand words, typed out on my phone, many too ugly to share here, because I cuss a lot when I'm angry. I went all the way back to my childhood, telling him how his strict rules, practically house arrest, had made me feel. I spit out the pain he had caused me in high school by not accepting me for who I am and trying to make me feel like there is something wrong with being gay. I skewered him for all the negative sermons he had dumped on me at Baylor and for never calling just to ask how I was doing. As I sat there furiously typing away, I felt like I had to purge myself of this awful bug that had been eating away at me for far too long.

And then I drove to the Ferrell Center, parked the Magnum, left the keys in it, and sent him one more message, telling him to come get his damn car because I didn't want it anymore. I couldn't help thinking about what had happened four years earlier, when I asked my teacher to follow me in his car so I could leave the Magnum at the clubhouse of our subdivision. Except this time I didn't need anyone to follow me. I just walked away.

I didn't deal with my dad for several days after that. I wouldn't answer his calls, and he knew better than to text me after everything I had said to him. But he texted my good friend Janell, knowing she would relay the messages to me. (Janell and I are tight from high school; I actually call her my sister, because she always has my back.) Dad was mad with how I was acting, and he said I was making a mistake about the car, that I would be stranded without it. He said the same thing to me when we started talking again. I said my friends would take care of me, and he made a dismissive sound, the equivalent of *Good luck with that*. He thought my expectations were too high, that my friends would end up disappointing me because they wouldn't be there for me.

But I had chosen my friends well at Baylor. And they came through for me when I needed them most, giving me rides to class, to practice, to games. I didn't even have to ask, which was a huge relief, because I don't like asking for favors. My bros Julio and Nash learned my daily schedule, and they would often be parked outside my last class, waiting to give me a quick lift to the arena for practice. Sometimes I would take my skateboard, but I usually wouldn't get more than halfway to wherever I was going before one of them would see me, pull a U-turn, and pick me up. All of my friends were amazing. Their response was the exact opposite of what my dad had predicted. Here I had concrete proof that much of what he had said over the years was the product of his own skewed worldview, and not necessarily reality. I wasn't alone in the world, with only him to protect me, which is how he had often made it seem. I was blown away by the realization that my Baylor friends were part of my family now too.

Sometimes I feel bad about all those text messages I sent to my dad. Then again, things are now better between us, so maybe it was a necessary, if painful, step. I said things that were mean and hurtful, but that was actually the first time in my life I had really said my piece to him—all of it, not just when I was sticking up for myself during one of his rants. Even in high school, when I moved out of the house for a while, our arguments had centered around my sexuality, and we stuck close to that topic. I defended myself when he said I was being influenced by other people, that I was just a follower. But I didn't bring up my childhood or tell him how some of his other paranoia made me feel.

My brother and sisters had their own run-ins with him; it was like a rite of passage. And when I unloaded on him in those texts and told him to take his car back, they weren't mad at me or disappointed. I think they were relieved in a way, almost as if they were wondering why it had taken me so long to exert my independence. "We were waiting on it, Baby Girl," DeCarlo told me. "We knew it was bound to happen."

WHEN I WOKE UP that morning, I had no idea the day would play out the way it did, that after blowing up at my dad, I would then take a big step forward in my friendship with Cherelle. She was a friend of a friend, and she had started hanging out with my group toward the end of my junior year. By November of senior year, we were all having barbecues a couple of times a week, usually at House 41, and "Relle" (as I often call her) would always be there. She struck me as steady and reliable; she had her head on straight. We would have good talks, and a few times I walked away from those dinners knowing there was something between us.

162   The day I got into it with my dad, I texted Cherelle and said, "You still going to dye my hair?" She had offered to color my hair at some point—I was always looking for people to help me out with that—and I felt like I needed to do something simple to calm me down and try to turn my mood around. She texted back and said, "Sure." But she didn't know I was heading over to her place right away. So when I showed up at her door a few minutes after getting her text, she started laughing.

She said, "I didn't know you meant now!"

And I said, "I thought that was my invite!"

As she worked on my hair, I started telling her about the things I had said to my dad. And the more I talked, the more I surprised myself. I don't often share something so personal like that, and certainly not with someone I don't know all that well. But midway through the night, I pulled out my phone and handed it to her. "I just sent these texts to my dad," I said. I also gave her the backstory, so she wouldn't think I was in the habit of being disrespectful to my parents. If anything, I've stretched a lot, and keep stretching, to make things right with my dad. We still bicker, and I'm not sure he has come to fully accept who I am, but we've been on pretty good terms since I left Baylor, because I think he has a better understanding of what lines not to cross.

When I left Cherelle's place that night, I knew she was somebody I wanted to be with, because I had opened up with her. She had a way about her that brought me out from behind the walls I had built. And the more time we spent together, the more sure I was that she had feelings for me, too. There was just one catch: she had never dated a woman before. At first I told myself we would just be friends. But eventually our mutual friends encouraged me to tell her how I felt, because they could see our connection and I was thinking about her all the time. So that's what I did. I texted her one day and said, "I really like you. And if you want to keep things the way they are, as friends, that's cool. I just thought you should know." She told me she respected my honesty, and that she liked the way things were between us. I knew she was going through a breakup, so I just kept acting the way I'd been acting, and she kept inviting me over to hang out.

One night, we were joking around after dinner, and Cherelle said, "You wouldn't put in the time to get me." She had a big smile on her face because she didn't think I would take her seriously. She was playing, but I wasn't.

"Oh yeah?" I said. "Just watch me."

She told me she wasn't convinced I would put in the effort to make things work, because she knew I had stopped trying with my previous girlfriend. She needed to know I truly cared about her, that I wasn't just looking for a fling. I had never chased a girl before—I was usually the one being pursued, or things just kind of happened—but I was more than willing to chase Cherelle and prove I was serious. I would meet her on campus after she got out of class, then walk her to the next one. Whenever we made plans, like going to the movies or chilling at her place, I'd show up early. I'd help with dinner, send her cute texts, make myself available as much as possible. Finally, after a couple of false starts (we'd get close, and then she'd pull back for a few days), she let her guard down and realized that being with me was something she wanted. We began dating toward the end of my senior year.

Getting close to Relle was a new kind of experience for me, my first adult relationship, one that was built on a solid foundation of friendship. Senior year was full of challenges, to say the least, but spending time with her helped me to look at things in a different way—and to express myself on a deeper level.

DESPITE THE BUMPY WAY our season started, with that loss to Stanford in Hawaii, we eventually cruised through the schedule, rolling up wins the way we had done during our run to the national championship. We were routinely beating teams, even really good teams, by double digits. But there was something different about the way we were winning. We had become a second-half team, occasionally finding ourselves in tight contests before pulling away down the stretch. Everybody was gunning for us because we were the defending champs, and the media loved asking, "Can anybody beat Baylor? Who can stop Brittney Griner?"

Senior Night at the Ferrell Center was one of the best nights of my life. I almost never get nervous before games. Even before the 2012 NCAA title game, I was really loose on our bus ride to the arena; I might as well have been on my way to a movie. But I've never been more nervous about a basketball game than I was on Senior Night. I couldn't quite comprehend that it was my last official home game, on the court where I had collected so many great memories. My emotions were all over the place. I was sad, uneasy, but also happy because I knew I had good things ahead of me. As I walked into the arena, I started thinking about all the little things I did before every home game, and then the scene played out just like it always did. I chatted with our support staff, listened to music in the locker room, laughed with my teammates. (Somebody was usually doing a crazy dance or acting silly.) Then I walked onto the court and said hello to our radio crew. I nodded and waved to the alumni who never miss a game. I spotted my bros, all the guys from House 41, screaming and yelling with excitement. Cherelle was there, too. Everything was the same, except now it all felt different, because I was looking at these familiar faces and thinking something I almost never think: *I don't want to mess up!* I'm usually pretty good about pushing negative thoughts out of my head when it comes to hoops. But that night, as we went through warm-ups and the clock ticked down to tip-off, I kept picturing myself having a terrible game, followed by this headline: "Brittney Griner doesn't score, fouls out on Senior Night." Every time that thought popped into my head, I told myself to go harder than I had ever gone before on the court.

And that's exactly what I did once the game started. We were playing Kansas State, a scrappy but undersized team, so I was trying to take advantage of my height in the paint. Once I got into the flow of the game, I just kept scoring and scoring. The more shots I hit, the more I wanted the ball. In the second half, I came out for a breather, and Shanay Washington leaned over to me and said, "You're over 35. Go get 40." I knew I had a lot of points, but I was still just focused on going hard, because K-State was knocking down threes and hanging around, keeping the score close. Then, during a break, Shanay said, "You're over 40. Go for 50." And that's when it really hit me, that I had a serious chance to score 50 points on Senior Night. We started to pull away with about nine minutes left in the game, but I was stuck on 46 for a while, because the Kansas State players were digging in, doing whatever they could to stop me. I heard one of them say, "Don't let her have it!" I scored with about three minutes left, and then thirty seconds later I hit my final bucket, on a fadeaway jumper after curling off two screens—the kind of shot I would almost never take. When it went in, I felt a huge sense of relief. I was running back on defense, and I gave Kim a look: *Okay, I'm all set! Get me out now, Coach!* She subbed for me, and the fans gave me an awesome standing ovation. As I walked to the sidelines, I saw Kim was crying, so then I started crying. She reached for my neck and pulled me down. (I was always hunched over talking to her, because she's only five foot four, so even when she's in four-inch heels, I still tower over her.) She patted me on the back and said, "What a game!" She paused for a second, then told me, "Soak all this in. You did it for your team and for the crowd. I love you." I nodded at her—that was all I could manage—and walked to the end of the bench.

166
    A couple of weeks later, we hosted the first and second rounds of the NCAA tournament, so we actually played two more games at the Ferrell Center. That was great for us, no doubt, but those games are run by the NCAA and they have a different feel than a regular Baylor home game. Our mind-set had shifted, too. Senior Night was a chance for everyone to show their appreciation—for the fans to thank us, for us to thank the fans—but now it was time for us to lock in and defend our crown. We were the No. 1 overall seed in the tournament, and we easily won our first-round game, 82–40. Two nights later, we played Florida State in the second round, and in some ways it felt like we were saying good-bye all over again, because this really was my last college game in Waco. While I was getting my ankles taped before the game, our radio guy, Rick, stopped by the training room and said, "Three dunks! That's how many you're going to get tonight. No woman has ever done that in a game before. You'll get it tonight."

I smiled and answered, "Okay, Rick!" Then, after he walked away, I shook my head and laughed, because people always say stuff like that to me. If some fans catch my eye as I'm walking onto the court, they'll shout, "Throw one down tonight, BG!" So I didn't think much about what Rick had said until I was jogging to the locker room at half time. We were winning big, 51–20, and I already had one dunk. I also felt like I had so much space in the paint that I'd get more opportunities to dunk in the second half. Florida State was a good team, but they didn't have a strong, physical inside presence, so I was able to get the ball deep in the paint and snag rebounds close to the rim. As I headed for the locker room, I started replaying what Rick had said: "You're going to get three dunks tonight!" And all of a sudden, I thought to myself, *You know what? He's right! That's exactly what I'm going to do!* The idea of it made me excited, knowing I could do something no other woman had done. But I let myself get caught up in the moment, and when I walked into the locker room at the break, I took my phone out of my locker and went to my Twitter page. I wanted to get the fans pumped for the second half, so I sent this tweet: "Need two more dunks on home court for the best crowd ever! #BaylorNation."

After I put my phone back in my locker, I started thinking maybe that wasn't the smartest move on my part, tweeting at half time. I had never done anything like that before, but it seemed so harmless, and I didn't think anyone would actually question my focus. I wanted to give myself a challenge. And later in the second half, I got my chance, dunking twice in the span of about a minute, right before Kim took me out of the game for good because we were already winning by so much. On the third and final dunk, I grabbed a rebound in the lane with three defenders around me and just went up and threw down a one-handed reverse. I think at other times in my career, I wouldn't have been

167

as forceful in my decision. I might have pump-faked, or turned and tried a little hook shot, because I sometimes worried about looking so powerful—which sounds ridiculous when I hear myself say it out loud. You think guys ever worry about that stuff? *I'm afraid to dunk this ball because people might think I'm too strong.* I can't imagine LeBron James ever has those thoughts in his head, but I did on occasion.

When Kim took me out, the crowd gave me an even bigger ovation than they did on Senior Night, and I gave her a big bear hug. I had chills. It was like another giant going-away party, except now we were heading to the Sweet Sixteen. Of course, once Kim found out I had tweeted at half time—because it was all over the news—she called me into her office the next day for another talk, telling me she would have to make an example out of me. She was clearly annoyed. "Big Girl, you know you're not supposed to do that," she said. "Now, when I start taking everyone's phones for this road trip, your teammates aren't going to be happy. But you have to take this one on your shoulders. You're the captain." Then she brought up something else: she said the media had been complaining about us, saying we disappeared after games when we were supposed to be available for reporters. And it was true. Most of us would hide in the back of the locker room as soon as our sports information director announced the door was opening for media. All of a sudden, everyone had to use the bathroom, or fix their hair, or they weren't feeling too good. We would drift away, and the reporters would just be standing around, waiting for us. So Kim said that was the real reason she was taking our phones away, because we needed to step up and deal with the media for the rest of the tournament.

This wasn't the first time she had tried to regulate our phone usage. Like a lot of coaches, Kim would occasionally collect our phones on road trips, and even sometimes for home games, in

168

an attempt to minimize distractions. When we were on the bus heading to an arena, she'd make us turn our phones in directly to her or an assistant coach. But we weren't stupid: we gave her old flip phones, or smartphones we had replaced with newer versions. And she wasn't dumb either: she knew those weren't our real phones. Also, even if I did turn in my real phone, I would still have had my iPad or laptop, so I could still get all my texts and e-mails, my Twitter and Instagram. The crazy part is that nobody said anything about this little phone game we played. Sure, we rolled our eyes because it was still a hassle, an extra step we had to take to get around the so-called ban, but we pretended like we took it seriously, and Kim pretended like we took it seriously. The whole thing was such a silly charade, all for show.

That didn't erase my mistake, obviously; I shouldn't have tweeted during the game. So I told my teammates what was coming, that my punishment would now be theirs, too. Most of them just said, "Really? Whatever." But a couple of them said, "Ugh, BG, why would you do that?" I reminded everyone that we didn't point fingers, that we were in it together, because all of us had messed up at some point. (Well, except for Makenzie. There's not much room for error when you're the coach's daughter.) They knew I was right, and there really wasn't anything else to say about it. When Kim met with us after practice that day, she announced she would be taking our phones again, because I had tweeted at half time.

The way we were playing, the way we were dominating, I don't think any of us were going to lose sleep over our phones. But if I had known what was waiting for us in Oklahoma City, I would have given Kim every piece of technology I owned.

THE LOSS TO LOUISVILLE

When I think about my last college game, the frustration and anger rush to the surface all over again, and my heart starts to race. It's like I'm still on that court in Oklahoma City, kneeling next to Odyssey Sims, wondering what the hell just happened. I went through so much at Baylor—the highs and lows of basketball, the highs and lows of trying to be myself—but I never imagined my career there would end the way it did. I never thought we would lose to Louisville, or anyone else, in the Sweet Sixteen of the NCAA tournament. We had gone 40-0 my junior year, and we were 34-1 heading into the Louisville game. I wasn't worried when we were down 10 points at half time, because we had been a strong second-half team all season. We always came back. Kim told us in the locker room,

"We dug this hole, and now we need to claw our way out." And we did. We were actually down 19 to Louisville with about eleven minutes left in the game, and then we made a huge run and took the lead by one point—until the refs called a terrible foul on me with two seconds left, and Louisville hit two free throws to go up again. Even then, I was thinking Odyssey would get the ball and make an amazing half-court shot to win the game.

When O's desperation heave hit off the backboard, I just froze for a moment. *Wait, what? This is it? It's over? This isn't happening.* I was so angry. I was angry at the refs. I was angry at Louisville. I was angry at myself. I just wanted to burst into tears right that second. But I told myself I had to be strong for my team and for O, because she was going through it hard, down on her knees, crumpled up on the court. She carried us that night, and now I needed to pick her up. I reached down for her arm and said, "C'mon, O, get up. We gotta shake their hands. Let's just do this, get off this court, and get back into the locker room."

I had so many emotions walking through that handshake line. I just kept telling myself to stay focused for one more minute so I could walk off the court and finish my college career with dignity. It wasn't easy. I was really heated. And now I had to walk through that line and congratulate Shoni Schimmel, their guard who had gotten in my face earlier. I felt like I could have slapped half the Louisville team, because that's what they did to me the whole game, and the refs didn't call it. But I also knew I didn't have my best game. I didn't take over like I should have taken over. I didn't keep my head in the game. The Louisville players were talking shit at me the whole time, and I let it get to me. This one girl in particular was going off, and finally I just let her have it. I said, "I'm going pro. I'm going to be the number one draft pick. What are you doing after college?" I mean, damn, being cocky like that is not even in my character. I was just so mad.

But, hey, credit Louisville. They had a game plan and stuck to it. They had two or three people hanging on me the whole time, following me everywhere I went on the floor, slapping my arms, elbowing me, pushing me. There is a picture from that game and it shows one of their players actually pressing her hand into my face. It was crazy physical. Their coach, Jeff Walz, was arrogant but smart. He knew I was basically playing with one arm tied behind my back. Ever since my freshman season, when I punched Jordan Barncastle, I had been careful about keeping my emotions in check on the court. Too careful at times. I didn't always play with the kind of fire I'm capable of—didn't demand the ball or get more physical when opponents pushed me around—because I was worried about crossing the line again. That's not something male players have to think about the way women do. We're judged by a different standard, as if there's something wrong with us if we lose our temper during the heat of competition. Let me tell you, I spent so much energy during that Louisville game battling my own emotions, it was almost like I didn't have enough strength left to step up and dominate. When Shoni Schimmel made that unbelievable reverse layup on me, then ran up in my face, yelling, there was nothing I could do. (She didn't say anything specific; she just let out a wild scream.) Some players probably would have pushed her away—and believe me, I was fuming on the inside. But I just had to pretend like she wasn't even there.

I did the same thing going through that handshake line. I was a zombie. As soon as I congratulated the last person, as soon as we were done with that line, I could feel the anger spilling over. I walked into the locker room and punched the whiteboard, the one that had our game plan written on it. I punched the lockers. I could have broken everything in that room. I had played by the rules, kept my cool, listened to my coaches at half time when they told me not to retaliate no matter what Louisville did. And what

173

did it get me? I just kept walking to the back of the locker room, into the bathroom, then sunk down in the corner and started bawling. I was crying so hard my body was shaking, and the tears were streaming down my cheeks.

I'll never forget that moment: sitting on the bathroom floor, my back against the wall, feeling like all the air had been sucked out of me. It was horrible. I actually went out that night and partied. Some people might not understand that, but when you lose a big game, on such a big stage, the last thing you want to do is go stew about it in your hotel room. So I just said screw it and went out with some friends. I wanted to forget everything. Of course, when I finally got back to my room late that night, I couldn't stop thinking about the game. I cried myself to sleep.

The next morning, everyone was texting me, but I didn't want to talk to anybody. I deleted my ESPN app from my iPhone and avoided TV. I didn't want to see the news about the game. On our bus ride to the airport, I put on my Beats headphones and drowned out everybody. It doesn't happen often, but when I'm feeling like that, there is really nothing anybody can say to make it better. I just need to deal with it myself before I can move on.

AS SOON AS WE LANDED in Texas, Kim told us all to meet in our locker room after we left the airport. Everyone was looking around and wondering, *Why are we doing this now?* In previous years, we didn't have our final team meeting until a few days after the end of the season, so we all had a chance to process everything before getting together one last time. But after the loss to Louisville, we headed straight from the plane to the gym, and when we got there, the coaches gave us bags so we could clean out our lockers. Then Kim said to us, "I know I probably won't see a couple of y'all anymore because you won't be around." I felt like those words were meant for me, so I said, "Who are you talking about?" And she looked at me and said, "I know you'll have things to do, the draft and all that, so you probably won't be around."

That stung me a little, the way she said it. She was right about my upcoming schedule—it turned out to be even crazier than I imagined—but I also felt like she was cutting ties with me right then and there, like I wasn't wanted around the program anymore. I was still reeling from the loss to Louisville, so I just put my head down, cleaned out my locker, and took all my stuff from the gym.

I didn't set foot in there again for weeks.

TWO DIFFERENT DIRECTIONS

I t's true what they say: winning cures all. At least, it was true for me and Kim at Baylor. Whatever frustrations we had with each other—the mistakes I made, the mistakes she made—all was forgiven after we won the national championship. Maybe it was only temporary amnesia, a four-month truce before we started clashing again at the beginning of my senior year. But when people looked at us, they saw something shiny and good, built on a sturdy foundation. And I can't help wondering what would have happened if we had won the title again in 2013, if that picture everyone had of us would still look the same way, with the two of us standing together, shoulder to shoulder, celebrating what we had accomplished.

But that's not what happened.

Cracks existed beneath the surface. And the game against Louisville, with the pressure cranked up, blew those cracks wide open. Before then, it was almost as if we had each made a silent pact to accept the other person's flaws in exchange for greatness, dominance, championships. I know I was challenging for Kim off the court, but she made it work because I played hard and helped lift her program to new heights. And while I struggled with some of her decisions, especially how she handled my sexuality, I respected her as a coach. When we stepped onto the court together, we made it work.

Except it didn't work in the Louisville game. Neither of us held up our end of the bargain. I didn't deliver the way I usually did, and she got outcoached. We both underperformed. We had created something magical for almost four years, and that night we watched, almost helplessly at times, as it melted away. We were left staring at all our warts and flaws, all the things about each other that drove us crazy. And we didn't have a national championship, the piece of shiny jewelry, to distract us from that reality. Kim and I were going in two different directions, and the game against Louisville was the fork in the road.

A few days after the loss, Kim tried to call me twice, but I didn't answer. I was still too raw, and I needed my space, some time to process what had happened and to get over the disappointment. But then I started hearing from some of my teammates that Kim was saying certain things about me, that I wasn't going to graduate, that I wasn't going to be around anymore. The way I heard it, I felt like Kim was bad-mouthing me, making it seem as if I was turning my back on the program because I had all these new obligations. Obviously, things get lost in translation, and I didn't know for sure what Kim had said or how she meant it, but at that point in our relationship, pretty much anything she said was going to send me down the rabbit hole. And once again, I allowed my emotions to get the best of me. I sent Kim a few texts telling her—not so nicely—to stop saying crap about me. (And, yes, I realize I might need to impose a twenty-four-hour rule for myself before I send text messages when I'm upset.)

I wasn't worried when she didn't write back. I had been taking her calls and her requests for meetings for four years (longer, actually, dating back to high school), so I just wanted a few days to take a deep breath and do my own thing. I figured we would reconnect at the Final Four, in New Orleans, maybe talk through everything that had happened. I had been named to the All-America team again, so I was scheduled to attend a ceremony and press conference there, not that I was looking forward to it. The last place I wanted to be was New Orleans, because the whole weekend was a reminder of our loss to Louisville, our stunning failure. While my Baylor teammates were as far away from basketball as they could get—except for Odyssey, who was also at the All-America awards—I was sitting on a folding table inside the press conference room at New Orleans Arena, my legs kicking off the sides, as I answered questions from the media for more than fifteen minutes. Guess what they kept asking about? *Why did you lose to Louisville? How will the program recover? What's next for Baylor?*

Many of the questions were ones that Kim should have been answering. Almost all college coaches attend the Final Four; it's basically a women's basketball convention. And Kim was the coach of the defending national champions, with two players being honored as All-Americans. But Kim wasn't in New Orleans. I don't know why she wasn't there. Maybe she was still angry or embarrassed about the Louisville game. She lost her composure down the stretch, ripping off her jacket at one point, and she blasted the refs in her press conference afterward. I didn't blame her one bit for that, but she was criticized in the media, and the NCAA later gave her a one-game suspension. Look, all of us were upset about the loss to Louisville, but I thought Kim could have swallowed her pride and joined me and Odyssey in New Orleans. Just one year earlier, Baylor had been the main attraction of the Final Four. So many people came to see us play, to see Kim coach, to see if we could finish the season undefeated. Now we couldn't even finish the season together. I felt abandoned, like I was no longer important because I was out of eligibility. Everyone kept asking me, "Where's Kim? How come Kim isn't here?" I just kept shrugging my shoulders. I didn't have a good answer for them.

EVERYTHING HAD BEGUN moving so quickly in the weeks after the Louisville game. I signed with an agent, Lindsay Kagawa Colas at Wasserman Media, who represents several WNBA stars, including my Mercury teammate Diana Taurasi and Maya Moore of the Minnesota Lynx. Lindsay's group works with action sports athletes, too, so that was a cool selling point for me, given my love of longboarding. I also knew I wanted to work with a woman, because I believe strongly in empowering women, and Lindsay understood I wanted to live openly and express myself freely. She totally got it. We agreed that if companies didn't want to endorse me because of my sexuality or my tattoos, then we didn't want to work with them anyway. We developed a blueprint for my future, which included a short-term plan, because the turnaround time between the end of the college season and the WNBA Draft is so quick, and it's crucial to capitalize on that window of relevancy. We were committed to being authentic, and we firmly believed that the right partners would want to work with us *because* of who I am, not in spite of it. The bottom line is that I don't want to pretend to be someone I'm not just to make some money. (I was happy the folks at Nike got that message too, signing me as their first openly gay athlete.)

I was still torn over leaving Waco, leaving my friends, but I was eager to show the world the real me, and to talk about more than just basketball or whatever topics Baylor deemed appropriate. I think the main reason I got tired of dealing with the media in college was because I got tired of hearing myself answer the same questions in the same way, over and over and over. I didn't feel like there was a lot of room to be all that interesting. It got to the point that during my senior year, every time I walked to the podium for media availability, I was hoping someone would finally ask me the big question: *Brittney, are you gay?* I knew it was never going to happen like that, but I would imagine it anyway, and how I would answer it. *Yes! I'm so glad someone finally asked! Yes, I'm gay!* Then I would have looked at Kim and watched her jaw drop. I resented those trips to the podium because I knew everyone would ask some version of the same three questions they always asked: *What's your mind-set? Is it tough having a bull's-eye on your backs? How do you keep from overlooking your opponents?* Blah, blah, blah.

I had set my sights on the WNBA while I was still in high school, once I started getting all the media attention and people were saying I was "one of a kind." Playing professionally became my dream, and the closer I got to the end of my college career, the more I thought about how I would feel hearing my name called at the WNBA Draft. And how I would look. After I signed with Lindsay, we talked about what I wanted to wear for the big occasion. She asked me, "Who do you admire? Whose style do you love?" As I was thinking about it, she mentioned Ellen DeGeneres, and my eyes lit up. Lindsay had a connection with Kellen Richards, the woman who styles Ellen, so she reached out to see if Kellen would be interested in designing an outfit for the draft. It wasn't an insignificant amount of money to spend, but Lindsay and I felt strongly that the draft was a significant moment for me, because I was stepping forward as my true, authentic self. Kellen put together a stylebook for me so I could pick out things I liked.

After we talked it over some more, she created a white tuxedo that I wore with white Chuck Taylor sneakers, and I loved the outfit so much that we worked with Kellen again for the 2013 ESPYs and for my cover shoot with *ESPN The Magazine*. (I also work with Jamie Steinfeld, a stylist based in Portland, Oregon.)

The morning of the draft, my alarm went off early, like 6 A.M., because I had a long day ahead of me. I was anxious, but mostly excited. The draft was being held on the ESPN campus, in Bristol, Connecticut, and I had a full slate of media obligations before the start of the draft broadcast that night: an appearance on *SportsCenter*, radio hits, a luncheon with other players and ESPN executives. Finally, toward late afternoon, all the draftees changed into our outfits for the evening; we had about an hour to prep before gathering for photo ops, doing meet and greets, and mingling with our families. My schedule had been packed all morning and afternoon, down to the minute, but now we had open hours to fill before the start of the broadcast. ESPN had set up a hospitality tent for friends and families, filling it with food, circular tables, and big-screen TVs. It almost looked like a wedding reception (perfect for my white tux).

My dad was there with a buddy of his, looking so proud and wearing a new suit of his own. I gave him a big hug. (The trip from Texas would have been too hard for my mom, but they both came to Phoenix later that week for my introductory press conference.) My bros Julio and Nash had flown in from Waco, and I was so excited to see them. They were grinning ear to ear, taking pictures with me and other draftees they had seen play over the years. I looked around at each table. I noticed Notre Dame coach Muffet McGraw was sitting with Skylar Diggins. I saw Tina Martin, Delaware's coach, with Elena Delle Donne and her family. At my table, Lindsay, my agent, was chatting with Lindsay Gottlieb, the head

182

coach at California, who had flown across the country with one of her assistants to support their star player, Layshia Clarendon. My head was on a swivel as I looked from table to table, expecting to see Kim sitting at one of them. I couldn't find her, but it was still early and I figured I would see her soon, at least get a chance to say hello before go-time. Whenever the door to that tent opened, I glanced over to see if she was walking inside. Meanwhile, I spent a big chunk of time talking to Texas A&M coach Gary Blair, who was there with his star post player, Kelsey Bone. That gave me a chuckle—good old Gary, still chatting me up, like he was trying to recruit me all over again.

The hours whittled down to minutes, and eventually it was time to leave the tent and walk to the studio where the draft would take place. As everyone expected, the Phoenix Mercury took me with the No. 1 pick. But much to my surprise, I was overwhelmed by the moment—I was so happy, I was speechless—and I stumbled through an on-camera interview. When that was done, an ESPN publicity staffer escorted me from the studio to the media press conference, which was on a different floor.

And that's when I happened to cross paths with Kim. We were walking along a hallway, and she seemed hurried. She quickly explained she was leaving, that she had a plane to catch. (I found out later from various people that she had entered the hospitality tent right before the draft started, then did an on-camera interview after Phoenix selected me.) She said congratulations and wished me good luck, and we posed for a few awkward photos. The whole interaction didn't last more than a minute or two. And it was only after she walked away that I thought to myself, *Wait, didn't she take a charter plane here?* (We always flew charters at Baylor.) I put the pieces of the puzzle together, and I came to the conclusion that she was leaving because she didn't want to stay, for whatever reason. It felt like she had shown up for the cameras, not for me. I remember walking away confused, as one of the Mercury staffers patted me on the back.

There is no right side or wrong side when it comes to Kim and me, just a lot of complicated feelings. I still love her. And I think she still loves me. But that interaction we had at the WNBA Draft, which happened simply by chance, would end up being the only time we spoke all spring, all summer, and into the fall, until just before I left to play overseas. I still text regularly with many people at Baylor, including some of the players, a couple of the assistant coaches, and most of the support staff. They would check in to wish me luck before Mercury games or congratulate me after big wins. My connection to the program still feels strong, even if Kim isn't at the center of it for me anymore. Whatever differences we have, whatever the distance between us, I'll always be grateful for what she taught me, and proud of what we achieved at Baylor.

184 We accomplished so much together.

WELCOME TO THE PROS

My Mercury teammates are great. I lived in the same apartment complex as Lynetta Kizer, Alexis Hornbuckle, and Charde Houston, and we all clicked right from the beginning of training camp. We just make each other laugh. They love to give me a hard time about my eating habits. Whenever I tell them I'm going to McDonald's, they say, "No! You need to get real food!" And I say, "That is real food in my book." At Jack-in-the-Box, I order the extreme sausage sandwich, with meat and cheese, no egg. I get it every time I go, no matter what time of day it is. I normally get two, but if I'm stopping there on my way to a game, I just order one sandwich, with an orange juice. I like things I can grab on the go—fast food, candy (love Skittles!), things that aren't exactly healthy. I've always been a picky eater. I found a few things I liked as a kid, and I've just stuck with them. My mom cooks the best ham ever. I also love steak. There's a place in Phoenix called Hillstone, and they have this amazing Hawaiian rib eye. It's got a little pineapple taste to it. Mmm . . . so good. But I know my teammates (and my agent) are right: I need to think more about the kinds of food I'm putting into my body. I'm trying to give vegetables a chance, so I'll order rice with peas and carrots in it. Baby steps.

I love the freedom of being a pro. I'm in charge of me now. Yes, more freedom also means more responsibility, but I'm learning how to handle it, even if the lessons are more expensive. During the first two months of my rookie season in Phoenix, the only reason I had been fined was for getting a couple of technical fouls. I could live with that, because I've come to realize it's better for me to show more emotion on the court, not less. Also, our best player, Diana Taurasi, had to pay some fines for jawing with the referees, so I felt like I was in good company. (She was actually suspended for two games by the league after getting her ninth technical of the season, which tells you what she thinks about the officiating.)

But on August 8, 2013, a little more than midway through our season, I got a serious introduction to life as a professional basketball player. The day before, I had bought a new iPad, and I spent the evening like most people would: playing with my new toy. Before I went to sleep, I set the alarm on my iPad and left it on my bedside table. I had to be at the arena at 8:30 in the morning for treatment with our trainer. I'd been battling knee and ankle injuries all season, missing games here and there, playing limited minutes, and I spent hours in the training room, trying to get the swelling under control. My alarm was supposed to go off at 7:45, which would give me a few minutes to snooze before getting up, throwing on a pair of shorts and a tank top, and making the quick drive to the arena, with wiggle room to spare. I hadn't been late for anything all season.

At some point that morning, Cherelle rolled over and said, all groggy and half awake, "Hey, what time is it? I think you need to get up." I heard her and mumbled an answer, saying I had set the alarm, and then we both drifted back to sleep. But she woke up again a little bit later. "This doesn't seem right," she said. "There's too much light outside." I sat up and looked at my iPad: It was 9:04 A.M.

"Oh my God!" I jumped up and scurried around the bedroom, collecting my things and tossing them into a bag. I was going so fast, I forgot my ankle was sore. Before I bolted out the door, I checked my iPad, and that's when I realized I had set the alarm for the wrong day. Such a rookie mistake. I flew to the arena, walking in the door an hour late, around 9:30. Our trainer looked at me, shook her head, and said, "I have to fine you. I'm sorry. I hate to do it, but those are the rules."

I wasn't worried about the money (it was a few hundred bucks), but I was disappointed in myself for making her wait. "Nah, I understand," I told her. "I'm the one who messed up."

Meanwhile, I had no idea that this was only the first twist in what would end up being a very long day.

A FEW MINUTES AFTER I got settled in to start treatment, our team president, Amber Cox, walked into the room. It wasn't unusual for her to be around, but what struck me was the look on her face, because she seemed upset. A second later, she said, "Everybody, go to the weight room right now." I walked into the weight room with a few of my teammates, and we waited for the others. Some of them were in the locker room, some already on the court shooting. Once we were all together, Amber told us to head to the film room that the guys, the Phoenix Suns, use. I thought that was strange. *Why are we switching rooms now?* I'm sure some of my older teammates figured out what was going on, but I was totally in the dark. Then the team owner, Robert Sarver (who also owns the Suns), walked into the film room, and that got everyone's attention. I'm thinking to myself, *What is going on here?* I looked around and saw the entire team was in the room, except for our head coach, Corey Gaines, and one of our assistants, Earl Cureton, who worked with me and the other post players.

Right about then, Mr. Sarver addressed us. "We let Corey go," he said. "We're getting a new coach, and he'll be in today." He went on to remind us that coaches are measured by how their teams produce, and we hadn't been producing the kind of results that were expected of us entering the season. We were 10-11 at the time, and inconsistent, losing to teams we should beat.

I had never experienced a coaching change before. At Baylor, Coach Mulkey was like a celebrity, and the program was so strong that I couldn't even begin to imagine her getting fired. Now I was sitting in that film room, trying to wrap my head around the news about Corey and Earl. My first emotion was disappointment, because I really liked both those guys, especially for who they are as people. Our team had been dealing with injuries, but I just kept thinking we needed to get on a roll and everything would work itself out. Obviously, management decided we needed a change, a different approach, to turn things around, and I could understand why when I really thought about it. My mind flashed back to our most recent game, a loss to the Seattle Storm, and how Corey had told us in the locker room beforehand, "They really want us to beat Seattle." He was trying to create a greater sense of urgency. But I don't think any of us knew just how serious it was—that if we didn't win, he would lose his job. He was in his sixth season as head coach, and the Mercury had won the WNBA championship with him in 2009. I just didn't see it coming at all, Corey being fired.

After the owner gave us the news, he asked, "Who's the captain?" Nobody said anything, because Corey had never officially named anyone captain. But Diana Taurasi—everybody calls her Dee—was always the one to talk with the referees at half-court before the start of our games, so Mr. Sarver looked to Dee and asked her to speak. She stood up. "We hate to see Corey and Earl go, but we also know you're right," she said. "This is a business. And we aren't winning."

We had started the season 0-3, which was a completely new experience for me. During my last two seasons at Baylor, our record was 74-2. So in about one week with the Mercury, I had dealt with more losing than in the previous two years combined. Wow. I didn't know how to handle it. *Losing? What is losing? What am I doing wrong?* And then I got hurt—first I sprained my left knee, then I rolled my right ankle—which was also a new experience for me. At Baylor, I didn't miss a game in four years, except for the two I sat out after punching Jordan Barncastle.

As we left the arena that day, I think we all knew it was time to look in the mirror. Corey had an up-tempo, run-and-gun style of play that we enjoyed, but we weren't accountable enough, especially on defense. We needed more discipline. I already felt like my first few months in Phoenix had been a crash course in life as a pro. But that meeting in the film room was when it really hit home for me, when I learned what happens when you don't produce.

Someone always pays the price.

EVEN BEFORE COREY WAS FIRED, I had gotten an interesting look at some of the behind-the-scenes business decisions that are important to the league. The one that really sticks out was a meeting that took place during my trip to Connecticut for the WNBA All-Star Game, at Mohegan Sun. Even though I had missed a bunch of games because of injuries, the fans voted me into the game, as the starting center for the Western Conference. I was really looking forward to playing, but my knee had other ideas, and the Mercury didn't want to take any chances. The league still wanted me to take part in All-Star weekend, though, because it's an important time to market our sport, and also a chance to hold meetings with a lot of the key players. So the WNBA flew me to Connecticut. (And by the way, for anyone who thinks life as a pro is glamorous for female ballers, I have some news: we fly coach class, and I was in a middle seat, missing those Baylor charter planes.)

The day before the game, in one of the conference rooms at the Mohegan Sun hotel, league executives showed us various designs under consideration for the new uniforms they're hoping to unveil for the 2015 season. But there was one problem: we didn't like what we saw. Apparently the idea is to come up with something more "appealing" to fans. What that means, of course, is that the designs were an obvious attempt to create something more traditionally feminine, to show our bodies in a way that will attract more men. Everything was tighter, more streamlined, and the shorts were even shorter than the ones we wear now. (I wore longer shorts in college.) There was actually an option to wear leopard-print tights beneath our shorts. I can probably think of a few women in the league who might like that look, but the bottom line is that the uniforms we saw won't flatter a lot of our players. We have some big girls in the WNBA, lots of different body types. A razorback jersey, essentially a track outfit, doesn't really work for a woman who is six foot four and 210 pounds. Not everybody in this league is stick-thin; most of us aren't. We care more about comfort on the court than sex appeal.

The league is trying to be edgier, but it feels like the marketing folks are still chasing a certain kind of fan—young men—who have never really watched the WNBA. (The fact that our league is supported by the NBA probably has something to do with that.) If we want to be edgier, we should focus more on finding clever ways to embrace the people who are more likely to attend our games, like the LGBT community, which has always been an important part of our audience. Heck, if you go to one of our Mercury games, you see all kinds of people in the stands: older folks, kids, gay men, straight men, lesbians, straight women, African Americans, Asians. What you don't see is the typical white-dude mainstream sports fan who shows up at football games wearing his favorite player's jersey. (Not that there's anything wrong with that.) Those guys don't care about women's basketball. So why do we keep trying to make them care? Not everyone has the same definition of sexy. And there's nothing sexy at all about having to wear something you don't want to wear.

Anyway, we were asked for our opinions in this meeting, and I didn't hold back. I said I thought the uniforms didn't work—not just the way they looked, but the way they felt, too. The top half of the jersey, up by the collarbone, was made from a different material than the bottom half, like an old-fashioned mesh, and while that might sound cool, it just doesn't absorb sweat. Also, it was see-through and thin. One hard foul down in the post would rip the material in half. (I suppose that would get more people watching us.) Other players voiced similar opinions. We were given a chance to try on the sample uniforms—I did it to be funny—but Diana Taurasi just shook her head and said, "I'm going to spend my summers on the beach in Hawaii while you're all wearing those things. Have fun."

On the morning of the All-Star Game, the players had breakfast with WNBA president Laurel Richie. She wasn't in the meeting the day before, when we saw the designs, so at one point she came up to me at breakfast and asked me what I thought about the uniforms. I told her, "I don't like them. They don't look like basketball uniforms anymore."

She got it. I think Laurel knew we weren't going to like those designs. They're still a work in progress, and hopefully our feedback will lead to something most of us can be happy with. We understand the need for a fresh look, but that doesn't mean we need to reinvent the wheel here. We've grown up playing in classic-style uniforms, so we're just looking for a functional, flexible design that allows each player to embrace and reflect her certain style—like you see in baseball, with some guys wearing their uniform pants long and baggy, and other guys going with the old-school, high-sock look. I like long, baggy shorts, and so do a lot of other players; some women like shorter shorts. The point is for us to be comfortable. Because you know what looks good on a basketball court? Players who are going all out, battling hard, doing everything they can to win.

192

A DOG NAMED DYLAN

I spent most of my first WNBA summer sharing my apartment with Cherelle before she returned to school at Baylor. We even adopted a dog together—at least temporarily. But I'm not sure Relle would use the word *we* because she thought I bought the dog for myself. As I've mentioned, I grew up with big dogs, and I thought about getting a pit bull when I left Baylor. But Relle wasn't much of a dog person before we met and didn't think she could handle such an intense breed right away, so we decided to compromise and start with a small dog. She looked around on-line and found one she thought she might like. Naturally, it was the tiny kind that you can fit into a teacup. I said I would buy it for her birthday, but once we officially decided to go ahead with it, that dog wasn't available anymore. In the meantime, I had been looking online too, and I found another dog, a miniature schnauzer with a chocolate coat. Diana's dog, Messi, is a mini schnauzer, and I thought it was kind of a cool breed. (He is named after soccer star Lionel Messi, because Dee is a huge soccer fan and her dad is from Argentina, like Messi.) When I asked Dee about her experience raising Messi the dog, she raved about how awesome he was.

So that's how it all began: the saga of Dylan, "cousin" of Messi. A couple of days before Cherelle's birthday, I bought Dylan from a breeder. He came with that name, and I thought it was cool, so I kept it. He was only about twelve weeks old, just old enough to go home with his new owner. I arranged to pick him up in Mesa, Arizona. Relle and I got into my truck and drove to the meeting spot. Everything seemed fine. I thought we were both happy to be adopting this puppy. After we collected Dylan, I climbed back into the driver's seat and put him on my lap. He was no more than five pounds. As we were pulling away, though, Relle suddenly burst into tears. I had no idea what was happening. That's when she told me she had been really excited about adopting a dog of her own, and she felt like I had gone back on my word. She said, "You bought yourself my birthday gift!" And she was leaning as far away from me as possible, almost like she wanted to climb out the window.

At this point, I just wanted to get the three of us home as quickly as possible. I was trying to make things right, but I kept saying all the wrong things, like asking Relle if we should stop at PetSmart, so we could get some stuff for Dylan. I thought maybe she would find it fun to buy him a bed and food, as a way for the two of them to start bonding. She couldn't believe I thought a visit to PetSmart would solve the problem. It sounds silly now, like most arguments do in hindsight, but she was really upset at the time, and I just wanted to make it better.

I was in the HOV lane, cruising along, not paying attention to my speed. All I wanted was to get home. But about halfway there, I saw flashing lights in my rearview mirror—and I panicked. Instead of pulling out of the HOV lane, across the other lanes, and idling on the right-hand shoulder, which is what I obviously should have done, I just pulled over onto the left side and turned off the engine. My truck was pinned up against the wall, with all the oncoming traffic zooming past us on the other side. The police officer was not happy with me for that. It was already bad enough that he clocked me going so fast. (Let's just say it was fast enough that I got summoned to show up in court.) I squeezed out of the front seat and met him behind the car, because the space was so tight I didn't think he could make it to my window.

"Where are you going?" he asked, clearly agitated.

"Phoenix," I said. "Home to my apartment." He called on his radio for another patrol car, for a second officer to come watch the traffic, because we were in a dangerous spot. He also kept calling me "buddy" and "pal," and it was obvious he thought I was a guy. When I was in high school and started dressing the way I wanted, wearing baggy jeans and hoodies, I would often get called "sir" or "buddy" or "dude." It happened a lot in the drive-through line at fast-food restaurants. The person working the window would see me on the low-res monitor, with my hoodie pulled up, and then I'd hear a voice coming through the speaker: "What can I get for you today, sir?" Back then, I ignored it. I wouldn't correct the person and say, "I'm not a sir." I would just roll with whatever was happening and place my order. I guess in those days, I didn't think I could have it both ways. I figured if I wanted to dress the way I did, I'd have to put up with people confusing me for a guy. But as I've gotten older, I've learned that some people are just lazy with their assumptions; they glance at your clothes and size you up without paying close enough attention to the person in the clothes. So now I correct people more often—unless I've just been pulled over for going almost twice the speed limit.

The second officer who showed up was much nicer. When he walked up to us, he mentioned right away how tall I am and asked if I was an athlete. I'm not in the habit of volunteering that information unless someone asks, but since he did, I said, "Yes, I play basketball." At the same time, I was handing over my license to the first officer. He took it, read my name, looked up at me, and said, "Thanks, ma'am," tapping the card against his wrist as he walked back to his patrol car with the other officer.

When he finally came back, he asked, "Why are you in such a rush?" I obviously wasn't going to explain exactly what was happening. *Well, see, my girlfriend and I went to pick up a mini schnauzer puppy from a breeder, but it turns out my girl is upset we got the dog, so I was just trying to get us home as quickly as possible before she starts crying again.* That didn't seem like a great idea. Meanwhile, Dylan is in the car with Cherelle, and I'm hoping they're bonding.

"Honestly, sir, I just spaced out," I said. "I wasn't paying attention like I should have been. I made a mistake."

The second officer had obviously helped him cool down. Eventually, the first guy issued me a ticket, while making sure to add, "I could have taken you to jail for this." I thanked him and said I would watch my speed. At this point, we had been pulled over for a long time, maybe half an hour. When I climbed back into the truck, I noticed the floor was wet. Turns out, Relle had tried to give Dylan some water by pouring it into the empty orange Tic Tac container that was in the cup holder.

Yep, this whole dog plan was going great so far.

I thought things would be better once we got back to my apartment, but I was wrong again. It wasn't just about Dylan. I had made big plans for Cherelle's birthday and booked a horse-and-carriage event that looked fun. I was even going to ride a horse

196

for the first time in my life, an idea that had always scared me. But after we picked up Dylan, and I picked up a hefty speeding ticket, I still had to get an MRI on my knee, so the doctor could see how my recovery was coming along. Obviously when I had scheduled the MRI, I didn't know everything else would get in the way. I thought Relle would be excited about Dylan. Instead, she couldn't even look at me, and she ended up canceling the carriage ride. So much of our summer already revolved around my WNBA schedule; this was supposed to be her special day, for once, and it managed to become about me again.

A few times over the summer, when Relle was particularly frustrated with me—like she was the day we got Dylan—she threatened to go back to Texas. That was her trump card. And on two occasions, I even booked a flight home for her, not so much to call her bluff, but because I'm not the type of person to try and change someone's mind if she's saying she'd be happier somewhere else. (In the end, Relle told me to cancel both tickets.) Another thing about me: I don't like going to bed knowing my girlfriend is angry at me. The night we got Dylan, Cherelle tried to sleep in the living room, but I couldn't sleep in the bed alone when I knew she was out there stewing on the couch. So I followed her into the living room and curled myself into a ball on the other end of the couch, because at least that way we could still be together. At first she wanted to get up and go back to the bedroom, leaving me there alone, but she knew I would just follow her again. And after a little while, when she saw how uncomfortable I was willing to make myself on that couch, trying to be near her and make things right, she finally gave up being mad at me and we went back to bed together.

It is also quite possible that Relle just wanted a good night's rest, because I was back in the doghouse the next morning when she realized I would be out of town for a week, traveling with the

Mercury, and she would have to take care of Dylan, who wasn't potty trained yet. He was just a tiny little thing, and he had no clue about where he should pee and poop. I had intended for Dylan to go to doggy day care when we brought him home, because I wanted people who actually knew what they were doing to start training him. But when I tried to take him to the facility that morning, they asked me if he'd been given all his shots, and of course he hadn't, which meant he couldn't join day care yet. So I put on my own puppy face (I'm told I have a good one), apologized up and down, and asked Relle if she would take care of Dylan while I was gone. She wasn't happy, obviously, but by this point I think she just wanted me out of her sight for a while, because she kept shaking her head and rolling her eyes. And it's not like I had given her any choice in the matter. We said our good-byes and I was out the door, on my way to meet the team bus at the arena, headed for the airport.

198   Dylan wasn't my first attempt at adopting a dog. My senior year at Baylor, I went to the local shelter with my roommate, Shanay, and we brought home a pit bull–dachshund mix. He seemed chill, well behaved—for a few days. Then one evening we went out, thinking everything would be fine, but when we got back later the apartment was a disaster area. The dog had chewed through a door, torn up furniture, and peed all over the place. I remember walking through the front door with Shanay, and we were both, like, "Oh, hell no!" So we returned the dog and got a snake instead. We realized we needed something that was contained, because we had so many obligations that took us away from the apartment for long stretches. (And yes, I might be a bit too spontaneous for my own good sometimes.)

Cherelle tried her best to train Dylan, but she had never worked with a puppy before, so she spent most of her time cleaning up after him. She actually taught him to poop in one corner of the patio, but he refused to pee outside. He would only pee inside the apartment. Relle was telling me these stories on the phone, and I just imagined the worst—Dylan peeing everywhere and Relle cursing my name the whole time. I pictured them in that apartment, miserable together. I also pictured having to go through the same thing myself when I got home, because Relle had her own trip planned. She was going to see her family for a few days.

A day after I got back to Phoenix, Cherelle left for Texas, and I quickly realized how hard it was taking care of Dylan. It doesn't help matters when it's 110 degrees outside. I was used to having dogs who stayed outdoors, dogs who had been potty trained by someone else. Working with Dylan was a big surprise, a serious challenge. And I was overwhelmed by it. That week, I had an appointment with the two women who do my hair. They're sisters, and I had met them during the photo shoot I did for *ESPN The Magazine* a couple of months earlier. We were on set for several hours that day, and they did an awesome job with my hair, making it look good in a bunch of different ways, so I started going to them on a regular basis. Now they were working on my hair, and I'm telling them about Dylan, and they're showing me pictures of their dogs. One thing led to another, and we made a plan for their family to adopt Dylan. It seemed like a great way out of a bad situation—definitely better for the dog. Cherelle had been upset when we got him, and I was worried about training him over the next few months. I didn't want us to keep fighting about him.

Before Relle returned from Texas, I gave Dylan to his new family. I thought everyone would be happier this way: Dylan, Relle, and me. And once again, I was wrong. I had made the decision on my own, without talking to Cherelle about it, partly because I figured she would be happy to come home and not have to deal with his mess again, but also because I felt like getting him had been a mistake, and I wanted to fix that mistake as quickly as possible. Unfortunately, I had also miscalculated Relle's attachment to Dylan.

"BG, where's Dylan?" Cherelle had just walked into the apartment, and she was looking around for the puppy.

"I found a new home for him," I said. "I gave him to a good family."

Her face fell. "You did what?"

I started to explain, but she put her hand up and said, "That's a house decision, BG. You can't just make a decision that affects the house without consulting me. I was looking forward to seeing him." She stared at me, then said it again: "That should have been a house decision."

The next day, Cherelle drove me to practice. When we pulled into the parking garage attached to the US Airways Center, I hopped out and went inside to get ready, while Relle sat in the car for a few minutes to make some calls. When Diana pulled into the garage, she spotted Relle and went over to say hello.

"How's it going?" Dee asked. "How's my baby Dylan?"

"Well," Relle told her, "Brittney gave him away while I was gone and didn't tell me."

"What?" Dee said. "I'm going to kick her ass."

"Can you slap her for me, too?" (Relle made sure to tell me about that part of the conversation.)

Dee smiled and said, "Yeah, I'm going right now," then jogged inside.

A few minutes later, Dee found me in the locker room and asked, "Where's Dylan?"

"Uh . . ." I wasn't sure what else to say, but it didn't matter.

"Your girl told me you gave him away!" If you've ever seen Dee jawing at a ref, then you know exactly what expression she had on her face: a wide-eyed, half-smiling look that says, *How could you be so stupid?!*

"He just wasn't working!" I said.

"I'm going to kick your ass," Dee said, shaking her head. "So Messi doesn't have a cousin anymore? They hardly knew each other!"

Needless to say, she didn't let me forget about that boneheaded play any time soon.

I really do want a dog of my own, but now I realize I want to adopt one who's at least a year old, and I'll have his shots done and send him straight to school for training. That's what we did when I was young; the dogs went to Man's Best Friend in Houston. My decision to get Dylan was just too impulsive. I obviously didn't think it through all the way. It felt right in the moment, but I didn't consider how a dog would affect my day-to-day life, and if I was ready for that kind of responsibility.

Technically, I'm an adult. But I'm still learning what that means exactly.

LESSONS OF A ROOKIE

When Russ Pennell took over as interim head coach of the Mercury, my teammates started cracking jokes with one another, saying things like "Hope y'all are ready to go back to college!" Everyone had gotten used to Corey's laid-back style, and now we would be playing for a guy who had spent his career in the college game, coaching men. But while most of my teammates had been in the league for several years, I had played my final college game only five months earlier. I was the baby on the team. So the idea of playing for a college coach—someone who would focus more on drills, on defense, on breaking down every little thing—didn't faze me one bit, even if the rest of them were saying, "Get ready to do defensive slides!"

Turns out, their jokes weren't that far off from reality. And that was a good thing. There was a definite college feel to the way Coach Pennell ran practices. During his very first practice with us (I was injured, so I couldn't play), he stressed that we were going to be playing more defense, better defense. I was happy to hear that. Defense was a huge part of our success at Baylor, so I was eager to see how we would get after it in Phoenix, now that someone was making it a priority for us to shut down other teams, not just outscore them. All jokes aside, we responded well to Coach Pennell. I think part of the reason was because we needed someone who could get the best out of us on both sides of the ball. But the other key was that he came into the situation with an open mind; he was ready to play anyone who showed him something. We had players on the roster who weren't seeing much court time, and they knew if they did the things he was asking, they would get on the floor. All of us wanted to prove ourselves. Nobody took anything for granted. It also helps when your best player is Diana Taurasi. She's the biggest competitor you'll ever meet, and she loves rising to the challenge, so if Dee is out there proving herself, the rest of us are going to fall in line. And if we didn't execute the way Coach Pennell wanted, he refused to look the other way. He would stop the drill, point out the problem, and tell you to fix it, even if he had to keep stopping the drill until everybody got it right. We all quickly realized we couldn't get away with anything sloppy. It was time for more accountability.

About two weeks after Coach Pennell took over, he called me out in the media. We lost to the Seattle Storm, and the two of us had a little chat after the game—and then he told the press exactly what he had told me. "Brittney has got to play better," he said. "We talked about greatness. We talked about what separates good from great. I think a lot of her adjustments are really what we go through from college to adulthood. All of a sudden, you have a job and you are expected to do your job well." I think some people assumed I would be annoyed by his words. It was the opposite, actually. He spoke the truth. I spent much of my WNBA rookie season letting somebody else take charge. We'd be on offense, and I would tell myself, *Dee will get that shot*, or I'd assume that Candice Dupree would make something happen, because she usually does. ("Pree" is so steady and smooth. She doesn't get the big spotlight, but she's automatic for 15 points a game.) I was settling way too much. And Coach Pennell called me out on it, which is what Coach Mulkey would do if I wasn't executing the way I should. I needed someone to say it out loud, and even to the media, so I could stop denying the reality of how I was playing.

For the final month of the WNBA season, I focused on asserting myself more on offense. That meant trying to set better screens, pin my defender on the block, demand the ball, and try to score. I had been floating around on offense, sometimes near the three-point line, nowhere near the basket when the shot was taken. My change in mind-set might not have been obvious on the stat sheet (I averaged 12.6 points a game as a rookie), but I believe it was the reason I hit the series-winning shot in Game 3 of the Western Conference semifinals, against the Los Angeles Sparks. If Coach Pennell hadn't prodded me to step up more, I probably would have tried to pass the ball when it ended up in my hands with just under seven seconds left in the game. And then I wouldn't have been talking afterward about my biggest moment as a pro—which also happened to be my sickest.

The morning of Game 3 against the Sparks, we had our team shootaround at the Staples Center, their home court. Afterward, we went back to our hotel and I ordered a steak from room service for lunch. I like my steak cooked medium-rare, but when this one arrived, it was more rare than usual. It tasted good, though, and I've eaten plenty of rare steaks before, so I polished it off without a second thought. I was feeling good, ready to go for the big game that night—until I walked into the arena. That's when the nausea hit. I started feeling horrible, but I didn't tell anyone because I was hoping it would pass. As soon as the game started, as soon as I jumped up for the opening tip, my stomach did a backflip. I knew right then and there that I had a tough couple of hours ahead.

I never ask to come out of a game, never ask for a quick breather, but at the first time-out, I raised my hand as I jogged off the court, then said to Coach Pennell, "I need one, right now. I need to come out." I think my teammates thought I was heading for the end of the bench, but I just kept chugging along, like Forrest Gump, all the way off the court and into the tunnel leading to the locker room—to the bathroom. About midway through the tunnel, my knee brace broke. One of the screws popped off the side, and the whole contraption came apart. I thought to myself, *This is a horrible look! I don't know who cursed me, but I am cursed right now.* I quickly made it to the toilet, then spent the next few minutes throwing up my pregame meal.

Our trainer, Tamara Poole, had followed me into the locker room. I said to her, "Tamara, I need some medicine. I'm queasy and my stomach hurts." We walked back out to the bench, where she gave me some antinausea medicine and I gulped down water. It wasn't long before Coach Pennell walked my way and asked, "You good?" I said, "Yup. Put me back in there." But I quickly discovered I wasn't good. As soon as I started running and jumping again, the next wave hit me. And this is how it went for the rest of the game, a back-and-forth battle with my stomach. I felt a little better during the third quarter and into the fourth, until the final minutes of the game, when I desperately wanted to run back to the locker room.

I was standing in the huddle before our final offensive possession, and I almost told Coach Pennell he needed to take me out. Instead, I took a deep breath and told myself I could handle it. I watched him draw up the play. We were down 77–76, with seven seconds left on the clock, and we had the ball along the sideline, on our end of the court, right in front of the Sparks' bench. DeWanna Bonner (aka "DB") was making the inbounds pass for us. I was supposed to set a screen to get Diana open, so she could catch the ball and take the final shot. And if Dee wasn't open, I was supposed to flash out and get the pass. I was nervous because DB had thrown me the ball from the same spot just a few plays earlier, and I had fumbled it out of bounds. As we were walking back onto the court to run the play that would decide our season, I said to Dee, "I'm going to set a mean screen and get you open." And in my mind, she was going to come off my screen, get the ball, hit the shot, and we'd all go crazy. *The Mercury win!*

That isn't how it happened, of course. The Sparks double-teamed Dee, so she wasn't open. As soon as I saw two defenders go with her, I knew what I needed to do. I had to get the ball and take the shot. We didn't have time for me to defer to someone else. And I had only one defender on me: Candace Parker. So I came back to the ball, and DB lobbed me a pass that led me toward the baseline. As I reached for the ball, I thought about the shot I always took at Baylor, my go-to move: turn toward my left shoulder, spin, face up, and release a soft little jumper. *Turn and shoot. Turn and shoot.* So when I caught the pass, I didn't even hesitate. I knew exactly what I was going to do.

When the ball went in, the Sparks immediately called time-out. My teammates were jumping up and down as we went into our huddle, but I was struggling, just trying to keep my insides from spilling all over the court. We still needed to make one more defensive stop, which we did, forcing Candace Parker into a long, off-balance shot. When the final buzzer sounded, I started running off the court. My teammates were shouting, "BG, doin' it for the rookies!" And I was yelling back, "Doin' it for the rooks!

Doin' it for the rooks!" Then I turned away and said, "And on that note . . . I'm heading to the bathroom!"

That night was one of the best moments of my life, if not exactly the prettiest. It was a great reminder that people sometimes perform their best when facing extra hurdles—like when I ran the timed mile in my Vans during my freshman season at Baylor. I honestly don't think I would have gone as fast in my running sneakers. And I needed that extra push from Coach Pennell after we lost to Seattle in August; I needed a reminder that the difference between good and great is something I must constantly look for within myself.

TOWARD THE END of my rookie season, I sat down with Coach Pennell and Mercury president Amber Cox to talk about my first summer with the team. They both left the organization a few weeks after the season, but our conversation that day has stayed with me, because they asked me the right questions. Was my rookie season a success? What things did I need to improve? How could I make sure that my second season would be better than my first? The bottom line is that I didn't have a great rookie run. Part of the reason was due to injuries. I had never missed games in college or even been slowed much because of injuries. But only a few games into my pro career, I sprained the MCL in my left knee. Then I rolled my right ankle, then my left ankle, and then my right ankle again. I even hurt my right shoulder at some point—I just woke up sore one day, not sure why—although I didn't miss any games because of it. Overall, I thought my first WNBA season was okay. I hate that I got injured early on, because I didn't want to be a disappointment. Everybody expected me to come in and take over, but I wasn't taking over. I didn't want people to think, *Oh, she's a flop*. I really struggled with that.

Even with the injuries, though, I know I could have played better. Amber and Coach Pennell essentially agreed with my "solid, but not great" assessment of my season. The three of us talked in Coach Pennell's office inside the US Airways Center. They told me I needed to demand the ball more on offense, and be forceful once I got it. They said I needed to focus on getting stronger, working on my core, adding weight to my frame. They also wanted to see me concentrate more on basketball. I was getting yanked every which way off the court. There were times, with all the media and public appearances I was doing—many of them at the request of the league—that basketball almost felt like an afterthought, and that my real job was trying to bring more attention to the WNBA. When we were on the road, I was always doing postgame appearances, which are required by my league contract. I wanted to say, on more than one occasion, "No, I can't do that," but people were telling me, "You're the face of the league now." I know the publicity stuff is important, as long as I can find the right balance. And figuring out how to make it all work is my responsibility. So it was good to hear Amber say we all need to be more selective going forward, that media and appearance obligations come second to hoops.

Later that afternoon, I also met with Lindsay, my agent. I asked her, "Can I have some time off after China?" She laughed and said, "Of course! That's already built into your schedule." Phew. She explained that when I returned from China, I would have a few solid weeks off before coming back to Phoenix in March to train at Athletes' Performance. (I met with some folks there when the WNBA season ended, and they did a movement analysis and a nutrition consultation for me, so I could try to get a jump on things in China.)

I felt much better after my conversations with Lindsay and my Mercury bosses that day, like I had the beginning of a good plan for how to make my second WNBA season better than my first.

MEANWHILE, MY ROOKIE YEAR wasn't over yet. In some ways, it was just starting again. After we lost to the Minnesota Lynx in the Western Conference finals, I had just a few days to catch my breath before heading to Las Vegas for a three-day training camp with USA Basketball. Then I spent the rest of October in Texas, squeezing in as much quality time as possible with my family in Houston, including my adorable little niece and nephew, and Cherelle in Waco before starting the next big chapter in my life: playing in China, for the Zhejiang Chouzhou Golden Bulls. (And yes, I had to find Zhejiang on a map after I signed my deal when I turned pro. It's about a two-hour drive from Shanghai.) Before Lindsay began negotiating with the team in Zhejiang, she asked me if I would feel more comfortable going to China, so far from home, if Nash and Julio could come with me. I said absolutely, so she built their travel and hotel into my contract. My boys had told me from the start, even before my first game with the Mercury, that they would take off a semester of school and go to China with me, because it's a once-in-a-lifetime opportunity. Knowing I would have a built-in support system gave me peace of mind, and my Chinese team agreed to put us all up in the same hotel for the winter, with me in one room and the bros in another: House 41 on the road.

I knew China would be an interesting challenge for me, on both a personal and a professional level. Cherelle couldn't come with us, because she was focused on finishing her prelaw degree at Baylor, and we were both a little nervous about navigating a long-distance relationship. At the same time, though, I was determined to make the most of my time playing abroad. Some of the WNBA's best post players would be spending the winter in China, too, including Sylvia Fowles (who's six foot six) and Liz Cambage (who's six foot eight), so I knew I'd face some serious competition. More than anything, I was ready to lock in, mentally, on becoming a better player, fine-tuning my body and skills for the professional game.

My contract with Zhejiang included salary and amenities for a personal coach, so while I was still in Phoenix, Lindsay set up interviews with three candidates interested in the job. She also asked Diana if she would sit in on the interviews because Dee had gone through the process before and would know the right questions to ask. But after we sat and talked with the first candidate, Dean Demopoulos, I decided to cancel the next two meetings. Dean was my guy—I was sure of it. He has been around the game for a long time, and worked as an assistant coach for three NBA teams, so he has an old-school, straightforward approach to certain things, which I liked when I met him. He didn't just talk about what we could do on the court; he said he wanted to get in the film room with me to watch video of my individual workouts, so we could study my footwork and fundamentals. I've always found that helpful. The more we talked, the more I realized he could help me a lot.

Everybody was asking me if I felt nervous about going to China. But I wasn't. I actually surprised myself a few times, telling people how much I was looking forward to it. (Well, except the part about changing my eating habits, which I'm trying to do.) I liked the idea of stepping away from the media spotlight for a few months and just focusing on basketball.

As I counted down the days before leaving for China, I kept thinking about everything that had happened over the previous twelve months since I was a college senior trying to hang on to the people and things I cared about while letting go of the pain and distractions that kept getting in my way. There was so much to process.

211

TWO WEEKS BEFORE FLYING ABROAD, I went back to Baylor for Homecoming weekend. I was excited, but also nervous about how some people might react toward me. I called the ticket office, and a friend of mine hooked me up with field passes for the football game. Before kickoff, I put on my sunglasses, flipped up the hood on my sweatshirt, and tried to slip onto the field unnoticed. Needless to say, that didn't work. I was standing on the sideline when I heard someone in the stands say, "Hey, that looks like Brittney!" I froze for a second; then I heard the crowd start to buzz. It was like a game of Telephone, as each person told the person next to them, pointing out where I was standing. So I took off my sunglasses and smiled. A few seconds later, everyone in that section started cheering, and I felt an overwhelming sense of relief wash over me as the fans waved and smiled back.

Of course, that wasn't the only hurdle I needed to clear while back in Waco. I had decided I wanted to reach out to Kim, to apologize for the texts I had sent her in the days after the loss to Louisville. No matter how much she had hurt me, much of the time unknowingly, I knew I could have behaved more respectfully toward her when my college career came to its abrupt end. So I stopped by basketball practice the day after the football game. All my former teammates were asking me, "You gonna talk to Kim?" She and I hadn't spoken in six months.

When she entered the gym, I walked over to where she was standing and patted her on the back.

"Hey, Coach," I said.

"Hey, Big Girl," she answered, offering a small smile.

"I'm going to come back tomorrow and talk to you," I told her.

"Okay. You know where to find me."

Two days later (I procrastinated because it was not going to be the easiest conversation), I went to Kim's office and found myself in that all-too-familiar spot: sitting across from her, separated by her desk.

"I came here to apologize for how I talked to you after the Louisville loss," I said. "That was wrong."

Kim nodded, but it quickly became clear that those texts were the least of her worries. The conversation shifted to the comments I had made in the media about the Baylor program and my frustration with the school's policy against homosexuality. Kim said she didn't understand why I had said all those things. She said I was making her look bad.

I shook my head. "I'm not trying to make you look bad," I said. "But when I talked about Baylor and the policy, and everything I felt when I played here, that was all true."

Kim insisted she had never said anything negative about me or asked me to take down any tweets. She said she wasn't mad at me, but that I needed to "set things right" at Baylor because I had created tension in the administration. She offered no apologies of her own, so I just simply repeated what I had said at the start, that I was sorry for the texts and for the bad blood. Then we talked a little bit more, about small stuff, and I gave her my new number. Before I left, she told me we would eventually be cool again, in a better place, but it would take time.

As I walked away from her office, I replayed our conversation in my head. What did it mean, to set things right with the administration? That felt like chasing a shadow. To make things right with school executives, I would have to accept their idea of what God believes. I would have to apologize for being me. Kim seemed to imply that I had betrayed Baylor, but whose Baylor did I betray exactly? Because my Baylor is made up of all the great friends I met in Waco, and the teammates I won a national championship with, and the fans who were cheering for me at the Homecoming game. I can't worry about somebody else's Baylor.

What I do wonder sometimes is how I can ever set things right with Kim if we can't have an honest, open conversation about the ways in which we've hurt each other. Maybe she's right that time will heal the wounds. Maybe she just needs longer than I do. All I know for sure is that I'm glad I went to her office that day, because it was time for me to move on.

I LEFT FOR CHINA on the first Sunday of November. When I walked out of my family's home, the sun hadn't come up yet, and the morning was chilly and dark. I placed my oversized bags in my red pickup truck and drove with my parents to the airport. We idled outside the drop-off area as I unloaded my stuff. I squeezed my mom tightly, rocking her back and forth. Then I walked over to my dad, and he wrapped me in a big hug. We stayed like that for a long time, cars streaming past us.

Finally he let go of me. He wiped his eyes. I nodded. Then I grabbed my bags and walked through the sliding glass doors.

It was time to see what was waiting for me on the other side of the world.

N ow everyone knows the real me, my strengths and flaws, my dreams and doubts, the whole story—my story. For so many years, it felt like I was folding myself into a cramped airplane seat (which is why I couldn't help but laugh at being stuck in the middle on my flight to the WNBA All-Star Game). There were times it seemed like no one had any real perspective on who I am, and some of that was my own fault. But now the plane has landed, and I've stood up and stretched out my arms and legs, and people can see all of me. I hope they also see how hard it was stuffing myself into a space that didn't quite fit me—how hard it is for anyone to do that.

Everything depends on perspective, and how much you're willing to let people know the real you. Some tall folks hunch over, trying to make themselves smaller. Some short folks wear heels, trying to make themselves taller. Me? I don't want a hurt back or sore feet. I want to walk along comfortably, content to let people think whatever they're going to think. I've learned, through a lot of trial and error, that the rewards of being authentic far outweigh the risks.

I have spoken my truth, and most people didn't run away from me. They weren't afraid of my sexuality, or my appearance, or my emotions, or my shortcomings. They weren't afraid of my desire to walk a different path from the one that society too often tries to choose for us all—the safe path. If I wanted to play it safe, I would never get out of bed in the morning. I stand out in the world, and I love that about myself. I didn't always feel this way, but I've come to discover that the more I embrace who I am, the more I connect with other people. And the more I connect with other people, the more I learn about myself.

Funny how that works, isn't it?

ABOUT THE AUTHORS

Brittney Griner was a three-time All-American at Baylor University, where she scored 3,283 career points (No. 2 in Division 1 women's history) and blocked 748 shots (No. 1 all-time), while earning national Player of the Year honors in both her junior and senior seasons. She lives in Phoenix, Arizona.

Sue Hovey is a former vice president and executive editor at ESPN. She spent fourteen years with *ESPN The Magazine* and is now an independent writer and editor. She lives in Brooklyn, New York.